No Fault
No Blame

**How to Reverse the Destruction
of Self-Esteem and Productivity
for Yourself and Your Family**

by

Claude R. Beamish

Illustrated by Debra Beamish

UNIQUE PRESS TACOMA, WASHINGTON

Printed in the United States of America.
Published by Unique Press, Tacoma WA 98402
Library of Congress Catalog Number 92-085287
ISBN 1-879243-07-5

For further information contact Claude R. Beamish, P.O. Box 2735, Gig Harbor, WA 98335.

Table of Contents

NOTE FROM THE AUTHOR

This book is based on scientific data and observable human behavior. The process presented and the results expected are based on the following brain processing pattern:

INPUT—THOUGHT—EMOTION—BEHAVIOR.

If you can change a person's thoughts about a subject or situation you almost immediately change that person's emotions and behaviors. The amount of change will depend on many factors covered in this book. What is offered here is not a cure-all, it is a tool.

How effective it is depends on how it is presented and whether or not the people involved see a need for change and whether they are unselfish enough to accommodate the needs of others.

The material in this book is meant to help people understand the causes and effects of their own behaviors and emotions. Because of a unique function of the human brain, using this material to try to change a spouse, child, or other person you are in conflict with will probably be counter-productive. The best approach to improve the relationship is to have the other person read the material for him/her self or for you both to attend a presentation of the material together.

When you read this book, try first to relate the information to your own life and behavior. Do not fall into the trap of attempting to evaluate other people with the objective of changing them.

Claude R. Beamish

INTRODUCTION

The Holistic View

At birth we all inherit a specific style of brain from our parents. This book was designed to give you access to the power that is contained within the type of brain you inherited. The kind of power that leaves you in the driver's seat when life accelerates, leaving you in control of your own responses in any situation. Not power that is used to dominate others, but the power to control our own lives in order to be happier and more successful. We need to stop being victims and stop victimizing others.

We must learn to look at unique brain usage patterns, sometimes called temperaments. Each of us falls into certain categories based on how our brains were designed from the moment of conception. We need to understand the natural function of the brain called Downshifting. This is a natural protective function of our brain which occurs when we are angry or upset.

We think that when we get angry or frustrated, it is the result of action occurring right then and there. Our minds are a swirl of activity. We know we're right and others are wrong. As our anger mounts, so does a sense of isolation, frustration, and sometimes blind rage. What if all those emotions were the result of our negative reaction to basic differences, between how we and those we are in conflict with, perceive the world? What if we all have different needs and expectations that are naturally the result of our specific brain's structure and usage patterns? Why do we get angry with others who are just living their lives the way their inherited brain judges is the right way to live? Unfortunately, we tend to take personally many things that are natural behaviors of others and which were not even intended to affect us at all.

There is ***No Fault and No Blame*** involved in how people act in anger or frustration when they are lacking the knowledge of how and why their brain functions the way it does. Unknowingly, we are each different and our brain slips into an angry mode so quickly that often we do not even know we are becoming angry or why. Learn why your brain is doing what it does and you will eliminate much stress and frustration from your life.

Brain Vocabulary You Need

A. *Downshifting* is a natural process, employed by the brains of humans and all other animals to handle situations involving anxiety and stress. This process includes the act of moving down to and using a different, and faster-acting older portion of the brain to react to a *perceived negative* situation. When this happens, our ability to control our life and learn is decreased.

The Basic Parts of the Human Brain

B. *The Neo-Cortex* is the upper and most advanced portion of the human brain. It has a right and left hemisphere. The two hemispheres are connected to each other and communicate to each other through a structure, made up of millions of connecting nerve fibers, called the *Corpus Callosum.* (See page 71)

C. *The Left Hemisphere* of the Neo-Cortex is the logical, verbal, math, and vocabulary oriented hemisphere.

D. *The Right Hemisphere* of the Neo-Cortex is the creative, nonverbal, art, and spatial oriented hemisphere.

E. *The Limbic System* or Old Mammalian Brain is located beneath the Neo-Cortex. It is the seat of basic natural drives and emotions. It is a faster-acting brain and where if not controlled, we downshift to, when we encounter stress. We cannot learn new information or have the control ability of the Neo-Cortex when we have downshifted to this portion of the brain.

F. *The Reticular Activating System* or Reptilian Brain is located beneath the Limbic System. It is the fastest acting portion of the brain. This area is basically responsible for handling involuntary body processes, screening input, and is where we downshift to in cases of severe crisis or anger when we are ready to fight or react in order to survive.

G. *Different Brain Hemisphere Functions*: The right and the left hemispheres of the brain handle the functions of Thought Processing, Perceiving, Evaluating, and Primary Brain Orientation in different and complementary ways. Most individuals use some combination of the right and left hemispheres together to handle these functions. But many individuals rely primarily on one hemisphere for certain functions.

Brain Function Definitions

H. *Thought Processing*: The act of the introverted, in depth, quiet, private right hemisphere; and/or the extroverted, cursory, verbal, gregarious left hemisphere; handling of thought processing.

I. *Perceiving*: The act of the all seeing, subconscious, laid back, expansive right hemisphere; and/or the limited, goal directed, intensely conscious left hemisphere; handling the viewing of the surroundings.

J. *Evaluating*: The act of the associative, comparing, questioning, extensive right hemisphere; and/or the logical, step by step, goal oriented left hemisphere; handling the evaluation of happenings in the environment.

K. *Primary Brain Orientation*: Having either the need or preoccupation of the right hemisphere; for processes or activities that are enjoyable; and/or the drive for task completion of the finish oriented left hemisphere.

L. *Brain-Caused Personality Traits*: The use of different combinations of the right or the left hemispheres to handle each of the above four different Brain Hemisphere Functions causes all of our different variable human abilities and personalities.

We are all different "on purpose." The variable brain capabilities and the personalities which accompany them allow people to fill all the roles in our society. Variations caused by different brain hemisphere strengths and weaknesses cause varying abilities, aptitudes, and attitudes. These variations allow humans to adapt to different environments, occupations, lifestyles, etc. The different brain organizations also cause an abundance of differing, and many times opposing, viewpoints and beliefs.

Separations and regroupings of individuals into groups of people because of vocational, philosophical, and religious tendencies, cause areas or regions in our cities, counties, and nation which are inhabited by higher percentages of people who all have similar brain hemisphere usage patterns. Since most people in these areas or even in similar occupations have similar beliefs and philosophies, they all tend to agree with each other. This continual agreement strengthens these people's convictions and decreases their ability and frequency of entertaining other ideas or philosophies differing from those they have learned to be "correct."

This tendency to have an inability or lack of desire to accept, listen to, or like the people who have differing brain hemisphere usage preferences is further complicated by the process called "Downshifting." This process is described in Leslie Hart's book, *Human Brain and Human Learning*. In his book, Hart states:

"... When the individual detects threat in an immediate situation, full use of the great new cerebral brain is suspended, and faster-acting, simpler brain resources take larger roles..."

Downshifting is a natural process, employed by the brains of humans and all other animals to handle situations involving anxiety and stress. This process includes the act of moving to and using a different, and faster-acting older portion of the brain to react to a "perceived" negative situation.

When you have that feeling of anxiety, anger, fear, etc., you have downshifted. It usually starts with what I described as the Repeating Tape. This is when your mind silently or you verbally start saying such things as: This isn't fair...They/you can't make me do it...They have no right...I don't have to...I don't like this...Why me?...I won't! At this stage you are at Level-One Downshifting. At this stage you cannot listen well to what other people are saying and you are unable to make decisions using your upper brain the way you could if you were not downshifted.

Persons who reach Level-Two Downshifting, could become violent and possibly not even remember what they have done. This is referred to as the Fight or Flight level of downshifting and usually leads to people regretting what they have done during this period.

Research shows that the control or lack of control over this function called downshifting, or just the act of avoiding situations causing downshifting, are the major factors which determine the level of development of the brain and its abilities. Also the level of productivity of a person or a group of people is directly related to the amount of control they have over the function of downshifting. The amount of control people have over downshifting is directly related to the amount of information on temperaments and downshifting they possess.

An Overview

People have varying Brain Usage Patterns because they are needed to be different to fill all the roles in our society. Disagreements over differences in needs, expectations, beliefs, philosophies, and ways of viewing and evaluating all cause people to downshift to varying levels. This downshifting derails the learning process and decreases productivity throughout our entire society.

What is a process we can use to reach a solution to this problem which causes so much hurt, anger, loss of self-esteem and productivity in our homes, schools, and businesses?

To begin with, we must complete the Sorter on pages 9 through 12 to see which hemispheres of the brain we use to view and react to the world.

Then you will read your individual profile, followed by descriptions of how individual portions of your brain function in order to create your special personality.

Next are the descriptions of the four Major Groups including the list of pitfalls (things that cause us to get angry) and controls for each. This section also includes similarities and differences which are caused by our inherited brain structure and the problems they cause.

Following the Four Major groups and the Pitfalls, there is further information on the brain and its structure including the concept of downshifting. The information in this section is designed to help you understand what is happening in our homes, schools, and businesses.

Once you have all the pieces of the puzzle, by using the self help section, you will be able to review how everything affects the schools, our children, families, businesses, and ourselves. In the self help section are other pieces of information to help you avoid problems and decrease anger, resulting in increased happiness and self-esteem for yourself and those around you.

Chapter 1
THE BRAIN HEMISPHERE USAGE SORTER

By choosing between nine pairs of opposing statements in each of the four parts the Brain Hemisphere Usage Sorter, the hemispheres you prefer to use for specific tasks can be determined.

The key to getting an accurate determination of which hemisphere or hemispheres a person uses in handling each of life's activities, is controlling the reasons why certain answers are chosen. We can have many reasons to answer questions in a particular way. Maybe someone is watching, a parent or teacher or spouse or anyone that we might feel would want us to answer in a special way. Many times in this situation we would choose answers different than those we would choose if the person were not present. Also the person answering the questions could be extremely angry or emotional.

The presence of extreme anger, emotion, or rebelliousness, or the act of answering questions to impress other people all invalidate the results of this sorter.

There are no correct answers to this sorter and it can only be valid and useful if you answer the way you really believe is right. The following mind set will be helpful in gaining accurate results. Choose your statements as if you have just won a 12 million dollar lottery, you are not married, no job, no kids, no responsibilities except to do things in the world the fairest way you can according to your own beliefs and natural behaviors. In other words choose the statements that are most like the real you or those that best describe how you really act, feel or believe.

There is a technique to help if you come to a pair of statements where it is hard to choose between the left and the right statement. Take a coin (this is not a joke) choose heads for the left statement and tails for the right statement. Then flip the coin. This decision making process is based on the concept that consciously we normally can only access one hemisphere when making decisions. The one we usually access is the conscious left hemisphere. It is basically impossible through pure thought to access the subconscious right hemisphere, since the right hemisphere normally communicates via feelings, hunches, or intuitions. One of the easiest ways to access our subconscious right hemisphere is to have an uncontrollable decision made by an outside force and then wait for the response, an emotional feeling which will validate or reject the decision. By knowing how the right hemisphere feels about specific decisions we can determine what it thinks. Since we do not have a control over flipping a coin, once the coin comes up either heads or tails an uncontrolled decision is made. Your right hemisphere will then respond with a strong feeling if it really agrees or disagrees. According to your feeling FOR (great!) or AGAINST (yuk!) as a choice determined by the coin flip, then either change your choice if your feelings disagree, or leave it if your feelings agree with the coin's result.

To be effective as a sorter, choices need to be made for all nine questions in all four parts of the sorter. Only nine answers may be chosen in each of the four parts of the sorter. Do not check both sides of any one question or leave both sides blank on any one question.

We are ready to start. Be as honest and true to yourself as you can when choosing statement A or B for all of the 4 sets of nine questions.

Part One

	A		B

1.___ I like to talk to few people; usually only people I know. OR ___ I like to talk to lots of people; even people I do not know.

2.___ I usually keep my feelings to myself. OR ___ I usually express or show my feelings.

3.___ I like to do projects by myself. OR ___ I like to do projects in groups.

4.___ I usually do not know what is happening in the lives of the people I know. OR ___ I usually know what is happening in the lives of the people I know.

5.___ I most often think quietly before I talk. OR ___ I most often talk as I am thinking.

6.___ When I am with a group of people, I most often wait for people to talk to me. OR ___ When I am with a group of people, I usually start the conversation.

7.___ It is easy for me to concentrate on homework even when the TV or radio is on. OR ___ I most often need a quiet place to do my work.

8.___ I like to think things over for awhile before I answer questions. OR ___ I most often start answering questions right away.

9.___ I would usually like to leave parties early because I get tired. OR ___ I would usually like to stay late at parties because they excite me and give me energy.

Total A

[   ]

Box #1

Total B

[   ]

Box #2

1   The Brain Hemishpere Usage Sorter

Part Two

A   B

1.___ I am usually most interested   OR ___ I am usually most
       in what is possible or what   interested in what is
       could be happening.   actually happening at the
                                                     moment.

2.___ People would say I have more   OR ___ People would say I have
       imagination.   more common sense.

3.___ I would more likely trust my   OR ___ I would more likely trust
       hunches.   my experience.

4.___ To me possibilities are more   OR ___ To me reality is more
       interesting.   interesting.

5.___ I usually work in spurts,   OR ___ I usually try to work
       rest, then start again.   steadily to completion.

6.___ I usually start putting things   OR ___ I usually read the
       together without reading the   directions first, then
       directions.   start putting things
                                                     together.

7.___ I am best at expanding ideas   OR ___ I am best at condensing
       and coming up with many   ideas and coming up with
       solutions.   one solution.

8.___ People would call me more   OR ___ People would call me more
       impractical and a dreamer.   practical and literal-minded.

9.___ When people are around, I   OR ___ When people are around, I
       am very aware of body language,   am usually only aware of
       facial expressions, body stance,   what they are saying.
       etc.

Total A   Total B

┌─────────────┐   ┌─────────────┐
│   │   │   │
└─────────────┘   └─────────────┘

Box #3   Box #4

Part Three

A

B

1.___   Emotion and caring are more important to me.

OR ___   Ideas and information are more important to me.

2.___   I usually make decisions based on likes and dislikes.

OR ___   I usually make decisions based on facts and information.

3.___   The lack of caring by other people bothers me most.

OR ___   The lack of knowledge and ability of other people bothers me most.

4.___   I would prefer a personal note about my work from my teacher or employer most.

OR ___   I would prefer to know what is right or wrong about my work most.

5.___   Disapproval by others bothers me most.

OR ___   Making mistakes or failing in front of others bothers me most.

6.___   Most people consider me to be more gentle and warm-heated.

OR ___   Most people consider me to be more firm and cool-headed.

7.___   I usually consider other people's feelings.

OR ___   Many times I do not consider other people's feelings.

8.___   I am most concerned with harmony and relationships.

OR ___   I am most concerned with truth and fairness.

9.___   I use lots of descriptions to explain what I know.

OR ___   I use few descriptions and get right to the point.

Total A

Box #5

Total B

Box #6

1 The Brain Hemishpere Usage Sorter

Part Four

	A		B

1.___   I like to have many options.   OR ___   I like to have decisions made.

2.___   The act of doing a project is most important to me.   OR ___   The act of finishing a project is most important to me.

3.___   I like changes.   OR ___   Too many changes bother me.

4.___   I start many projects, but sometimes don't finish them all.   OR ___   I work on a few projects one at time and usually finish them all.

5.___   Sometimes I am late getting to where I am supposed to be.   OR ___   I am almost always on time and sometimes even early.

6.___   I often wait to the last minute to do an assignment or job.   OR ___   I usually plan ahead to finish my assignments or jobs.

7.___   I do not like schedules and routines.   OR ___   I like schedules and routines.

8.___   I usually just let things happen in my life.   OR ___   I plan, organize, and run my life.

9.___   I enjoy being surprised about what is going to happen.   OR ___   I want to know what is going to happen before it happens.

Total A

Box #7

Total B

Box #8

Scoring

Add up the number of statements chosen in each of the A and B columns for each page of the sorter. Put the totals in the numbered boxes at the bottom of each column.

Determining Your Profile Letters

When all four of your Brain Hemisphere Function Usage letters are combined together, a complete profile can be developed which will describe your needs, desires, aptitudes, and behaviors.

To do this refer to the results of the sorter and the following lettered and numbered boxes. Use scratch paper if you wish.

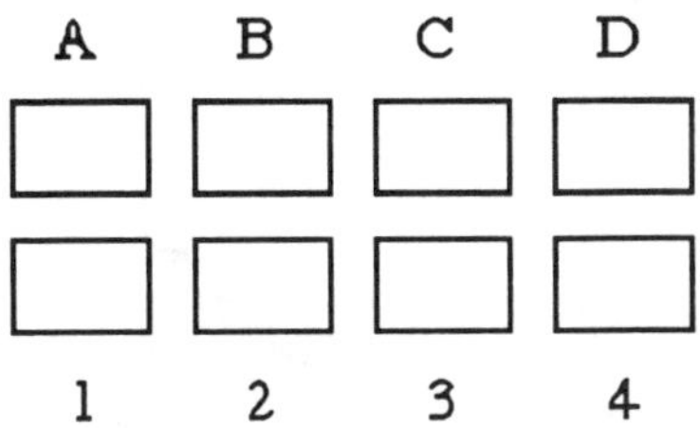

Look at your results in boxes 1 and 2 on page 9, put the highest number score (5, 6, 7, 8, or 9) in box A above. If the score is highest in box 1, (on page 9) put an I for Introvert in box 1 above. If the score is highest in box 2, put an E for Extrovert in box 1 above.

On page 10, look at your results in boxes 3 and 4, put the highest number score (5,6,7,8, or 9) in box B above. If the score is highest in box 3, put an N for Intuitor in Box 2 above. If the score is highest in box 4, put an S for Sensor in box 2 above.

On page 11, look at your results in boxes 5 and 6, put the highest number score in box C above. If the score is highest in box 5, put an F for Feeler in box 3 above. If the score is highest in box 6, put a T for Thinker in box 3 above.

On page 12, look at your results in boxes 7 and 8, put the highest number score in box D above. If the score is highest in box 7, put a P for Process Oriented in box 4 above. If the score is highest in box 8, put a J for Finish Oriented in box 4 above.

Use the letters in boxes 1,2,3, and 4 above as your Temperament or Profile letters. It would be helpful for you to write your letters and numbers on a piece of scratch paper or on your bookmark so you can refer to them readily as you read the following chapters.

1   The Brain Hemishpere Usage Sorter

Put your score in this form on your paper.

SAMPLE: <u>8</u>   <u>8</u>   <u>5</u>   <u>8</u>
             I   N   T   J

Here are what the letters stand for in most other books on this topic. The only ones changed were the P and J.

1. I   Introvert
2. E   Extrovert
3. N   Intuitor
4. S   Sensor
5. F   Feeler
6. T   Thinker
7. P   Process oriented
8. J   Finish oriented

Chapter 2
THE SIXTEEN PROFILES

When all of the left hemisphere temperament letters (ESTJ) are chosen, all of the left hemisphere temperament functions are predominantly in use and all of the left hemisphere characteristics are enhanced. A person is rule and finished oriented, into-the-moment, and thinks in a very logical, goal-directed manner. Organizing, controlling, detailing, and managing are enhanced abilities.

When all of the right hemisphere temperament letters (INFP) are chosen, all of the right hemisphere temperament functions are predominantly in use and all of the right hemisphere characteristics are enhanced. A person is of a perceiving and questioning nature and there are usually no absolute truths. Finishing tasks and coming to a conclusion could be a problem. Thought is random and possibility-oriented. Artistry, creativity, caring, and problem solving are enhanced abilities.

Instead of having all left or all right hemisphere temperament letters or preferences, most people have genetically directed preferences for combinations or blends of left and right hemisphere functions such as (ENFP), (INFJ), (ENFJ), (ISFP), (ESFP), (ISFJ), (ESFJ), (INTP), (ENTP), (INTJ), (ENTJ), (ISTP), (ESTP), and (ISTJ). Make sure your letters match one of these or the ESTJ or INFP presented above. These different combinations or blends of hemisphere temperament functions cause an abundant amount of different specific types of abilities, philosophies, and behaviors in people.

The accuracy of your profile which is presented next is determined by the strength of your scores. The closer your four numbers above the four letters are to 9,9,9,9, the more accurate your profile will be. If you have scores closer to 5,5,5,5, your profile, since you have characteristics of both hemispheres, will be close, but some characteristics will not be as strong.

Use your four Temperament letters on the following Index to find your Personal Profile.

Profile Index		Page No.	Profile Index		Page No.
a	INFJ	17	i.	ISTP	33
b.	ENFJ	19	j.	ESTP	35
c.	INFP	21	k.	ISFP	37
d.	ENFP	23	l.	ESFP	39
e.	ESTJ	25	m.	INTJ	41
f.	ISTJ	27	n.	ENTJ	43
g.	ISFJ	29	o.	INTP	45
h.	ESFJ	31	p.	ENTP	47

If your four letters do not match one of the above sets of letters, you may have made a mistake in scoring. Go back and rescore your results.

a. INFJ

The INFJ person is a very private person. When thinking, you are quiet and it may seem to others that you are in a different world. You gain energy by finding quiet times away from people.

You have an inquisitive quick mind. You have the ability to see in and around situations or problems. It is highly probable that you have artistic talents. You have the ability to come up with many possible answers to problems. Since you are an Intuitor you will daydream a lot. Because of this, you will sometimes drift off in thought, forgetting what you were doing.

Because of the NF combination, you worry about other people and their problems. You base your decisions in life on the basis of past experiences, your likes and dislikes, and the impact your decisions will have on others. To the Thinkers of the world, your decisions may be considered illogical and inconsistent. You could have a tendency to take on too many of the problems of your family, friends and acquaintances, thus becoming tired, over-burdened and stressed out, or causing them to be irritated and stressed out. You also worry about how other people feel about you.

Since you have an intuitive mind that always questions, you probably continually question your own self-worth. You need people to express verbally their caring and support for you. You also need people to think and express that you are a good person and that what you do is valuable.

You are driven to finish your projects or jobs whether you enjoy them or not. If you do not like a project anymore, you may need to decide that the project can be eliminated or you may finish it anyway, just so you don't have to worry about it. The J in your personality gives you the ability to be on time and plan ahead. You basically have the attitude of doing things because they need to be done. Your feeling of pleasure comes more from finishing the project than the act of doing the project.

Being a quiet, private, caring, and finish-oriented person, you will fit in almost anywhere. However, you are much happier in situations or occupations that involve problem solving or the arts where you do not have to deal with too many people for too long.

When people do not meet your needs and expectations, you will have a tendency to downshift into anger. When downshifted, you will become emotional (mostly hidden), with a more hawk-like behavior, just waiting for the problem to happen again. The emotion for the most part will not be expressed immediately, but will be stuffed deep inside and will only be released when the last straw breaks the camel's back. The following giant outburst of anger will be surprising to the people present. They will probably not even know about all of the continual little things that accumulated to cause the outburst. When downshifted, your personality will probably change to a rule and regulation type of person, worrying about whether other people finish things in the appropriate way. People might say you have a chip on your shoulder when you are downshifted. Of all the temperaments this is the one which, after recovering from downshifting, will always come back and help try to straighten out the problem in order to help people.

As with all temperaments your natural qualities are needed in society. Your specific brain organization is only found in approximately 2.4% of the female population and .8% of the male population. You probably have had a difficult time finding people who think and act like you do. Growing up with few people to validate and support your beliefs and behaviors could have left you with an undeserved low self-esteem.

All in all, when happy, you are naturally a very valuable, quiet, caring, problem solving, finish oriented, and loving person. Continue on page 49.

b. ENFJ

The ENFJ person is outgoing and needs to be with people. When thinking, you probably will be talking at the same time. Your world is the outer world of activities with people. You gain energy by being with people.

You have a quick inquisitive mind with the ability to see in and around situations or problems. You are able to come up with many possible answers to problems. Because of this characteristic, you may find it hard to accept authoritarian black or white answers. You are an Intuitor and daydream a lot. You sometimes drift off in thought and forget what you were doing.

Because of the NF combination, you worry about other people and their problems. Your decisions in life are made on the basis of past experiences, your likes and dislikes, and the impact your decision will have on others. To the Thinkers of the world, your decisions may be considered illogical and inconsistent. You could have a tendency to take on too many of the problems of your family, friends, and acquaintances, thus becoming tired, over-burdened and stressed out, or causing them to be irritated and stressed out.

You also worry about how other people feel about you. Since you have an Intuitive mind that always questions, you will probably continually question your own self-worth. You need people to verbally express their caring and support for you. You also need people to think and express that you are a good person and that what you do is valuable.

You are driven to finish your projects or jobs whether you enjoy them or not. If you do not like a project anymore, you may need to decide it can be eliminated, or you may finish it anyway, just so you don't have to worry about it. The J in your personality enables you to be on time and plan ahead. You basically do things because they need to be done. Your feeling of pleasure comes more from finishing a project, than the act of doing a project.

Being this out-going, caring, and finish-oriented person, you will fit in almost anywhere. However, you are much happier in situations or occupations involving problem solving, dealing with people.

When people do not meet your needs and expectations, you have a tendency to downshift into anger. When downshifted you will become emotional (expressed both verbally and possibly physically), with a more hawk-like behavior, just waiting for the problem to happen again. When downshifted your personality will probably change to a control and regulating type of person, worrying about whether other people finish things in the appropriate way. When downshifted you might also change to a very rule oriented style and try to solve your problems through the process of making rules to control others. People might say you have a chip on your shoulder when you are downshifted.

As with all temperaments, your natural qualities are needed in society. Your specific brain organization is found in approximately 7% of the female population and 2.4% of the male population. Because of this, you may have had a difficult time finding people who think and act like you do. Growing up with few people to validate and support your beliefs and behaviors could have left you with an undeserved low self-esteem.

All in all, when happy, you are naturally a very valuable, out-going, caring, problem solving, plan ahead, and task completion loving person. Continue on page 49.

c. INFP

The INFP person is a very private person. When thinking you are quiet and it may seem to others that you are in a different world. You gain energy by finding quiet times away from people.

You have an inquisitive quick mind. You can see in and around situations or problems. It is highly probable that you have artistic talents. You are able to come up with many possible answers to problems. Since you are an Intuitor, you daydream a lot. Because of this, you sometimes drift off in thought and forget what you were doing.

Because of the NF combination, you worry about other people and their problems. Your decisions in life are based on past experiences, your likes and dislikes, and the impact your decisions will have on others. To the Thinkers of the world your decisions may be considered illogical and inconsistent. You could have a tendency to take on too many of the problems of your family, friends and acquaintances, thus becoming tired, overburdened and stressed out, or causing them to be irritated and stressed out. You also worry about how other people feel about you.

Since you have an intuitive mind that always questions, you probably continually question your own self-worth. You need people to express verbally their caring and support for you. You also need people to think and express that you are a good person and that what you do is valuable.

You have little need or wish to finish the projects you like, since you enjoy them so much. If you do not like a project anymore, you probably will just eliminate it. The P in your personality lets you be spontaneous and flexible. Basically your attitude is to do things that you like to do and only finish the other projects if the reward is great enough.

Being a quiet, private, caring, and an activity oriented person, you will fit in almost anywhere. However, you are much happier in situations or occupations that involve problem solving or the arts where you do not have to deal with too many people for too long.

Your biggest problem is following through and finishing tasks. People of other personalities might see your natural behaviors as flighty and unrealistic.

When people do not meet your needs and expectations, you tend to downshift into anger. When downshifted you become emotional (mostly hidden), with a more hawk-like behavior, just waiting for the problem to happen again. The emotion for the most part will not be expressed immediately, but will be stuffed deep inside, only to be released when the last straw breaks the camel's back. The following giant outburst of anger will be surprising to the people present. They will probably not even know about all of the continual little things that accumulated to cause the outburst. When downshifted your personality probably changes to a more freedom and don't-tell-me-what-to-do-style. People might say you have a chip on your shoulder when you are downshifted.

As with all temperaments, your natural qualities are needed in society. Your specific brain organization is found in, approximately, only 2.4% of the female population and .8% of the male population. Because of this, you probably have had a difficult time finding people who think and act like you do. Growing up with few people to validate and support your beliefs and behaviors could have left you with an undeserved low self-esteem.

All in all, when happy, you are naturally a very valuable, quiet, caring, problem solving, spontaneous, and activity loving person. Continue on page 49.

d. ENFP

As an ENFP person, you are outgoing and need to be with people. When thinking, you probably will be talking at the same time. Your world is the outer world of activities with people. You gain energy by being with people.

You have an inquisitive quick mind able to see in and around situations or problems, and to come up with many possible answers to problems. Since you can see so many possible solutions to problems, you may find it hard to accept authoritarian black or white answers. This could lead to having a difficult time getting along with other people if you continually express your opposing views. Since you are an Intuitor, you daydream a lot, and sometimes drift off in thought and forget what you were doing.

Because of the NF combination, you worry about other people and their problems. Your decisions in life are based on past experiences, your likes and dislikes and the impact your decisions will have on others. To the Thinkers of the world, your decisions may be considered illogical and inconsistent. You could have a tendency to take on too many of the problems of your family, friends, and acquaintances, thus becoming tired, over-burdened and stressed out, or causing them to be irritated and stressed out. You also worry about other people's feelings about you.

Since you have an intuitive mind that always questions, you probably continually question your own self-worth. You need people to express verbally their caring and support for you. You also need people to think and express that you are a good person and that what you do is valuable.

You have little need or wish to finish the projects you like, since you enjoy them so much. When you do not like a project anymore, you probably will just eliminate it. The P in your personality enables you to be spontaneous and flexible. Basically your attitude is to do things you like to do and only finish other projects if the reward or pay is great enough.

Being this out going, caring, and activity oriented person, you will fit in almost anywhere as long as you are not downshifted. However, you are much happier in situations or occupations involving problem solving and dealing with people.

Your biggest problem is following through and finishing tasks. People of other personalities might see your natural behaviors as flighty, argumentative, and unrealistic.

When people do not meet your needs and expectations, you have a tendency to downshift into anger, becoming emotional (expressed both verbally and possibly physically), with a more hawk-like behavior, just waiting for the problem to happen again. When downshifted, your personality probably changes to a more freedom and don't-tell-me-what-to-do style. People might say you have a chip on your shoulder when you are downshifted.

As with all temperaments, your natural qualities are needed in society. Your specific brain organization is found in approximately 7% of the female population and 2.4% of the male population. Because of this, you may have had a difficult time finding people who think and act like you do. Growing up with few people to validate and support your beliefs and behaviors could have left you with an undeserved low self-esteem.

All in all, when happy, you are naturally a very valuable, out going, caring, problem solving, spontaneous and activity loving person. Continue on page 49.

e. ESTJ

The ESTJ person is outgoing and needs to be with people. When thinking you may be talking at the same time. Your world is the outer world of activities with people. You gain energy by being with people.

You have an orderly and organizing mind. You feel the need to set up rules and regulations in order to gain control over situations or problems. You are able to set up procedures and systems so that things will flow smoothly. Everything seems to have black or white answers.

Being a T you are very good at arguing and debating. You may tend to explain the correct way of doing things to others. Doing this, you could end up being continually angry with others and having them continually angry with you.

Since you are a Sensor you are strongly connected to the present and you worry about your control over it. You base your decisions in life on facts, information, and the logical outcome. To the Feelers of the world, your decisions may be considered inflexible, cold-hearted, and pushy.

You have a strong need for fairness and things happening the "Correct" way. Because of this, you may tend to get involved in the problems of your family, friends, and acquaintances, thus becoming irritated and stressed out or causing them to be irritated and stressed out.

You are driven to finish your projects or jobs, whether you enjoy them or not, and when you do not like a project anymore, you may need to decide that it can be eliminated, or you may finish it anyway, just so you don't have to worry about it. The J in your personality enables you to be on time and plan ahead. You basically have the attitude of doing things because they need to be done. Your feeling of pleasure comes more from finishing, than the act of doing the project.

Being this out going, organizing, finish, and control oriented person, you will fit in almost anywhere if you don't get too pushy. However, you are much happier in situations or occupation involving managing, controlling, or organizing, dealing with people or information.

When people do not meet your needs and expectations, your tendency is to downshift into anger. When downshifted you become very angry and argumentative (expressed both verbally and possibly physically), with a more hawk-like behavior, just waiting for the problem to happen again. When downshifted your personality probably changes to an even more rule and regulation type of person, worrying about and watching to see whether other people finish things in the appropriate and correct way. When downshifted, with this rule oriented style, you might try to solve your problems through the process of making more rules and procedures to control others. This might only lead to worsening the problems. People might say you have a chip on your shoulder when you are downshifted.

As with all temperaments, your natural qualities are needed in society. Your specific brain organization is found in approximately 21% of the male population and 7% of the female population. Because of this, you might of had a difficult time finding people who think and act like you do. Even though you might not admit it, growing up with few people to validate and support your beliefs and behaviors could have left you with an undeserved low self-esteem.

All in all, when happy, you are naturally a very valuable, out going, organizing, plan ahead, task completion, and managerial oriented type of person. Continue on page 49.

f.   ISTJ

The ISTJ person, is a very private person. When thinking you are quiet and it may seem to others that you are in a different world. You gain energy by finding quiet times away from people.

You have an orderly and organizing mind. You feel the need to set up rules, regulations, and procedures in order to gain control over situations or problems. You are able to set up procedures and systems so that things flow smoothly. Everything seems to have black or white answers. Being a T you are very good at arguing and debating.

You could have a tendency to explain the correct way of doing things to others. Doing this, you could end up being continually angry with others or having them continually angry with you.

Since you are a Sensor, you are strongly connected to the present and worry about your control over it. You base your decisions in life on facts, information, and the logical outcome. To the Feelers of the world, your decisions may be considered inflexible, cold-hearted, and pushy.

You have a strong need for fairness and for things happening the "Correct" way. Because of this you could have a tendency to get involved in the problems of your family, friends, and acquaintances, thus becoming irritated and stressed out or causing them to be irritated and stressed out.

You are driven to finish your projects or jobs, whether you enjoy them or not. If you do not like a project anymore, you may need to decide it can be eliminated, or you may finish it anyway, just so you don't have to worry about it. The J in your personality lets you be on time and plan ahead. You basically have the attitude of doing things because they need to be done. Your feeling of pleasure comes more from finishing, than the act of doing the project.

Being this quiet, organizing, finish, and control oriented person, you will fit in almost anywhere if you don't get too pushy. However, you are much happier in situations or occupations involving managing, controlling, or organizing, dealing with facts or information away from large groups of people.

When people do not meet your needs and expectations, you tend to downshift into anger. When downshifted you become emotional (mostly hidden), with a more hawk-like behavior, just waiting for the problem to happen again. The emotion for the most part will not be expressed immediately, but will be stuffed deep inside, only to be released when the last straw breaks the camel's back. The following giant outburst of anger will be surprising to the people present. They will probably not even know about all of the continual little things that accumulated to cause the outburst. When downshifted your personality probably changes to an even more rule and regulation type of person, worrying about and watching to see whether other people finish things in the appropriate or correct way. When downshifted, with this rule oriented style, you might try to solve your problems through the process of making more rules and procedures to control others. This might only lead to worsening the problems. People might say you have a chip on your shoulder when you are downshifted.

As with all temperaments, your natural qualities are needed in society. Your specific brain organization is found in only 7% of the male population and 2.4% of the female population. Because of this, you may have had a difficult time finding people who think and act like you do. Even though you might not admit it, growing up with few people to validate and support your beliefs and behaviors could have left you with an undeserved low self-esteem.

All in all, when happy, you are naturally a very valuable, quiet, organizing, plan ahead, task completion, and managerial oriented type of person. Continue on page 49.

g. ISFJ

The ISFJ person is a very private person. When thinking you are quiet and it may seem to others that you are in a different world. You gain energy by finding quiet times away from people.

You have an orderly and organizing mind. You feel the need to set up rules and regulations in order to gain control over situations or problems. You are able to set up procedures and systems so that things flow smoothly. Everything seems to have black or white answers.

Being an F you base your decisions in life on past experiences, your likes and dislikes, and the impact your decisions will have on others. To the Thinkers of the world, your decisions may be considered illogical and inconsistent. You could have a tendency to explain the correct way of doing things to others. Doing this, you could end up being continually angry with others and having them continually angry with you.

Since you are a Sensor, you are strongly connected to the present and worry about your control over it. You base your decisions in life on your feelings of how you think things should be. You have a strong tendency to worry about people and to make sure things happen the "Correct" way.   Because of this, you tend to get involved in the problems of your family, friends, and acquaintances, thus becoming irritated and stressed out or making them irritated and stressed out.

You are driven to finish your projects or jobs whether you enjoy them or not. If you do not like a project anymore, you may need to decide that the project can be eliminated or finish it anyway, just so you don't have to worry about it. The J in your personality lets you be on time and plan ahead. You basically have the attitude of doing things because they need to be done. Your feeling of pleasure comes more from finishing, than the act of doing the project.

Being this quiet, finish, control, and caring oriented person, you will fit in almost anywhere if you don't get downshifted. However, you will be much happier in situations or occupations involving managing, controlling, or organizing, dealing with facts or information away from large groups of people.

When people do not meet your needs and expectations, you tend to downshift into anger. When downshifted you become very emotional (mostly hidden), with a more hawk-like behavior, just waiting for the problem to happen again. For the most part this emotion is not expressed immediately, but is stuffed deep inside, only to be released when the last straw breaks the camel's back. The following giant outburst of anger will be surprising to the people present. They probably do not even know about all of the continual little things that accumulated to cause the outburst. When downshifted your personality probably changes to an even more rule and regulation type of person, worrying about and watching to see whether other people finish things in the appropriate and correct way. When downshifted, with this rule oriented style, you might try to solve your problems through the process of making more rules and procedures to control others. This might only lead to worsening the problems. People might say you have a chip on your shoulder when you are downshifted.

As with all temperaments, your natural qualities are needed in society. Your specific brain organization is found in only 7% of the female population and 2.4% of the male population. Because of this, you might of had a difficult time finding people who think and act like you do. Even though you might not admit it, growing up with few people to validate and support your beliefs and behaviors could have left you with an undeserved low self-esteem.

All in all, when happy, you are naturally a very valuable, quiet, organizing, plan ahead, task completion, managerial, and caring type of person. Continue on page 49.

h. ESFJ

The ESFJ person is outgoing and needs to be with people. When thinking, you probably talk at the same time. Your world is the outer world of activities with people. You gain energy by being with people.

You have an orderly and organizing mind. You feel the need to set up rules and regulations in order to gain control over situations or problems. You are able to set up procedures and systems so that things will flow smoothly. Everything seems to have black or white answers.

Being an F you base your decisions in life on the basis of past experiences, your likes and dislikes, and the impact your decisions will have on others. To the Thinkers of the world, your decisions could be considered illogical and inconsistent. You could have a tendency to explain the correct way of doing things to others. Doing this, you could end up being continually angry with others or having them continually angry with you.

Since you are a Sensor, you are strongly connected to the present and worry about your control over it. You base your decisions in life on your feelings of how you think things should be. You have a strong tendency to worry about people and to make sure things are happening the "Correct" way. Because of this, you could have a tendency to get involved in the problems of your family, friends, and acquaintances, thus possibly becoming irritated and stressed out or causing them to be irritated and stressed out.

You are driven to finish your projects or jobs whether you enjoy them or not. If you do not like a project anymore, you may need to decide that it can be eliminated, or finish it anyway, just so you don't have to worry about it. The J in your personality lets you be on time and plan ahead. You basically have the attitude of doing things because they need to be done. Your feeling of pleasure comes more from finishing, than the act of doing the project.

Being this out going, finish, control, and caring oriented person, you will fit in almost anywhere if you don't get downshifted. However, you will be much happier in situations or occupations that involve managing, controlling, or organizing dealing with facts or information and groups of people.

When people do not meet your needs and expectations, you tend to downshift into anger. When downshifted you become very angry and argumentative (expressed both verbally and possibly physically), with a more hawk like behavior, just waiting for the problem to happen again. When downshifted your personality probably changes to an even more rule and regulation type of person, worrying about and watching to see whether other people finish things in the appropriate and correct way. When downshifted, with this rule oriented style, you might try to solve your problems through the process of making more rules and procedures to control others. This may only lead to worsening the problems. People might say you have a chip on your shoulder when you are downshifted.

As with all temperaments, your natural qualities are needed in society. Your specific brain organization is found in approximately 21% of the female population and 7% of the male population. Because of this, you might have had a difficult time finding people who think and act like you do. Even though you might not admit it, growing up with few people to validate and support your beliefs and behaviors could have left you with an undeserved low self-esteem.

All in all, when happy, you are naturally a very valuable, out going, organizing, plan ahead, task completion, managerial, and caring type of person. Continue on page 49.

i. ISTP

The ISTP person is a very private person. When thinking you are quiet and it may seem to others that you are in a different world. You gain energy by finding quiet times away from people.

Your mind is very much locked into the present. You have a greater ability to concentrate on what you are doing than most other people. It is highly probable that you work with tools of some sort, or you are in some into-the-moment process that you enjoy.

Because of the SP combination, being into-the-moment and into doing activities you enjoy, you have a great need or drive to be able to do what you want to do when you want to do it.

You base your decisions in life on facts, information, and the logical outcome. To the Feelers of the world, your decisions may be considered inflexible, cold-hearted, and pushy.

You have a strong need for fairness, freedom, and for things to happen the "Right" way. Because of this, you tend to get involved in the problems of your family, friends, and acquaintances, thus becoming irritated and stressed out or making them irritated and stressed out.

You have little need or wish to finish the projects you like, since you enjoy them so much. If you do not like a project anymore, you probably will just eliminate it. The P in your personality lets you be spontaneous and flexible. Basically you have the attitude of doing things that you like to do and only finish the other projects if the reward is great enough.

Being a quiet, logical, and activity oriented person, you will fit in almost anywhere as long as there are not too many rules or situations that are too controlling. However, you may be much happier in situations or occupations that involve activities centered around tools, a process you enjoy, or arts or craft work, where you do not have to deal with too many people for too long of a time.

One big problem is following through and finishing tasks. Another big problem is dealing with too many rules or controls on your need for freedom. People of other personalities might see your natural behaviors as flighty, unrealistic, and possibly selfish.

When people do not meet your needs and expectations, you tend to downshift into anger. When downshifted you become very emotional (mostly hidden), with a more hawk-like behavior, just waiting for the problem to happen again. The emotion for the most part is not expressed immediately, but stuffed deep inside, only to be released when the last straw breaks the camel's back. The following giant outburst of anger will be surprising to the people present. They probably do not even know about all of the continual little things that accumulated to cause the outburst. When downshifted your personality probably changes to an even more freedom and don't-tell-me-what-to-do style for yourself and to a more rule orientation and controlling style toward others. People might say you have a chip on your shoulder when you are downshifted.

As with all temperaments, your natural qualities are needed in society. Your specific brain organization is found in, approximately, only 7% of the male population and 2.4% of the female population. Because of this, you may have had a difficult time finding people who think and act like you do. Growing up with few people to validate and support your beliefs and behaviors could have left you with an undeserved low self-esteem.

All in all, when happy, you are naturally a very valuable, quiet, logical, freedom loving, spontaneous, and activity loving person. Continue on page 49.

j.   **ESTP**

The ESTP person is outgoing and needs to be with people. When thinking you probably talk at the same time. Your world is the outer world of activities with people. You gain energy by being with people.

You have a mind very much locked into the present, and a greater ability to concentrate on what you are doing than most other people. It is highly probable that you work with tools of some sort or in some into-the-moment process that you enjoy.

Because of the SP combination, being into-the-moment and into doing activities you enjoy, you have a great need or drive to be able to do what you want to do when you want to do it.

You base your decisions in life on facts, information, and the logical outcome. To the Feelers of the world, your decisions may be considered inflexible, cold-hearted, and pushy. You have a strong need for fairness, freedom, and for things to happen the "Right" way. Because of this, you could tend to get involved in the problems of your family, friends, and acquaintances, thus becoming irritated and stressed out or making them irritated and stressed out.

You have little need or wish to finish the projects you like, since you enjoy them so much. If you do not like a project anymore, you will probably just eliminate it. The P in your personality enables you to be spontaneous and flexible. You basically have the attitude of doing things that you like to do and will only finish the other projects if the reward is great enough.

Being the out going, friendly, logical, and activity oriented person, you will fit in almost anywhere as long as there are not too many rules or situations that are too controlling. However, you are much happier in situations or occupations involving activities centered around tools, a process you enjoy, or arts or craft work where you can interact with lots of people.

One big problem is following through and finishing tasks. Another big problem is dealing with too many rules or controls on your need for freedom. People of other personalities might see your natural behaviors as flighty, unrealistic, and possibly selfish.

When people do not meet your needs and expectations, you tend to downshift into anger. When downshifted you become very emotional (expressed both verbally and possibly physically), with a more hawk-like behavior, just waiting for the problem to happen again. When downshifted your personality probably changes to an even more freedom and don't-tell-me-what-to-do style for yourself and to a more rule orientation and controlling style toward others. People might say you have a chip on your shoulder when you are downshifted.

As with all temperaments, your natural qualities are needed in society. Your specific brain organization is found in approximately 21% of the male population and 7% of the female population. Because of this, you may have had a difficult time finding people who think and act like you do. Growing up with few people to validate and support your beliefs and behaviors could have left you with an undeserved low self-esteem.

All in all, when happy, you are naturally a very valuable, out going, logical, freedom loving, spontaneous, and activity loving person. Continue on page 49.

k. ISFP

The ISFP person is a very private person. When thinking you are quiet and it may seem to others that you are in a different world. You gain energy by finding quiet times away from people in the outdoors.

You have a mind very much locked into the present. You have a greater ability to concentrate on what you are doing than most other people. It is highly probable that you work with tools of some sort or in some into-the-moment process that you enjoy.

Because of the SP combination, being into-the-moment and into doing activities you enjoy, you have a great need or drive to be able to do what you want to do when you want to do it.

You base your decisions in life on past experiences, your likes and dislikes, your own special needs, and the impact your decisions will have on others. To the thinkers of the world, your decisions may be considered illogical and inconsistent. Because you care, you could have a tendency to get involved in too many of the problems of your family, friends and acquaintances, thus becoming tired, over burdened and stressed out. Being an Introverted Feeler, you also worry about how other people feel about you.

You have little need or wish to finish the projects you like, since you enjoy them so much. If you do not like a project anymore, you will probably just eliminate it. The P in your personality gives you the ability to be spontaneous and flexible. Basically your attitude is of doing things that you like to do and you only finish other projects if the reward is great enough.

Being a quiet, private, caring, and activity oriented person, you will fit in almost anywhere as long as there are not too many rules or situations that are too controlling. You are much happier in situations or occupations that involve activities centered around tools, a process you enjoy, or arts or craft work, where you do not have to deal with too many people for too long.

One big problem will be following through and finishing tasks. Another big problem will be dealing with too many rules or controls on your need for freedom. People of other personalities might see your natural behaviors as flighty, unrealistic, and possibly selfish.

When people do not meet your needs and expectations, you tend to downshift into anger. When downshifted you become very emotional (mostly hidden), with a more hawk-like behavior, just waiting for the problem to happen again. The emotion for the most part is not expressed immediately, but is stuffed deep inside, only to be released when the last straw breaks the camel's back. The following giant out-burst of anger will be surprising to the people present. They probably do not even know about all of the continual little things that accumu-lated to cause the outburst. When downshifted your personality proba-bly changes to an even more freedom and don't-tell-me-what-to-do style for yourself and to a more rule orientation and controlling style toward others. People might say you have a chip on your shoulder when you are downshifted.

As with all temperaments, your natural qualities are needed in soci-ety. Your specific brain organization is found in, approximately, only 7% of the female population and 2.4% of the male population. Because of this, you probably have had a difficult time finding people who think and act like you do. Growing up with few people to validate and sup-port your beliefs and behaviors could have left you with an undeserved low self-esteem.

All in all, when happy, you are naturally a very valuable, quiet, car-ing, freedom loving, spontaneous, and activity loving person. Continue on page 49.

I.   ESFP

The ESFP person is outgoing and needs to be with people. When thinking, you probably will be talking at the same time. Your world is the outer world of activities with people. You gain energy by being with people.

You have a mind very much locked into the present. You have a greater ability to concentrate on what you are doing than most other people. It is highly probable that you work with tools of some sort or in some into-the-moment process that you enjoy.

Because of the SP combination, being into-the-moment and into doing activities you enjoy, you have a great need or drive to be able to do what you want to do when you want to do it.

You base your decisions in life on past experiences, your likes and dislikes, your own special needs, and the impact your decisions will have on others. To the Thinkers of the world, your decision may be considered illogical and inconsistent.

Because you care, you could tend to get involved in too many of the problems of your family, friends and acquaintances, thus become tired, over burdened and stressed out or causing them to be irritated and stressed out. As an Extroverted Feeler who is into enjoying yourself, you make the perfect party person. Being a Feeler, you also worry about how other people feel about you.

You have little need or wish to finish the projects you like, since you enjoy them so much. If you do not like a project anymore, you probably will just eliminate it. The P in your personality enables you to be spontaneous and flexible. You basically have the attitude of doing things that you like to do and will only finish the other projects if the reward is great enough.

Being an out going, friendly, caring, and activity oriented person, you will fit in almost anywhere as long as there are not too many rules or situations that are too controlling. However, you are much happier in situations or occupations that involve activities centered around tools, a process you enjoy, or arts or craft work, where you can interact with lots of people.

One big problem is following through and finishing tasks, and another is dealing with too many rules or controls on your need for freedom. People of other personalities might see your natural behaviors as flighty, unrealistic, and possibly selfish.

When people do not meet your needs and expectations, you tend to downshift into anger. When downshifted you become very emotional (expressed both verbally and possibly physically), with a more hawk-like behavior, just waiting for the problem to happen again. When downshifted your personality probably changes to an even more free-dom and don't-tell-me-what-to-do style for yourself and to a more rule orientation and controlling style toward others. People might say you have a chip on your shoulder when you are downshifted.

As with all temperaments, your natural qualities are needed in society. Your specific brain organization is found in approximately 21% of the female population and 7% of the male population. Because of this, you may have had a difficult time finding people who think and act like you do. Growing up with few people to validate and support your beliefs and behaviors could have left you with an undeserved low self-esteem.

All in all, when happy, you are naturally a very valuable, out going, caring, freedom loving, spontaneous, and activity loving person. Continue on page 49.

m. INTJ

The INTJ person is a very private person. When thinking you are quiet and it may seem to others that you are in a different world. You gain energy by finding quiet times away from people.

You have an inquisitive quick mind. You are able to see in and around situations or problems, and to come up with many possible answers to problems. Since you can see so many possible solutions, you may find it hard to accept authoritarian black or white type of answers.

Being a T you are very good at arguing and debating. You could tend to continually express your disagreements with others, or to correct others. Doing this, you could end up being angry with others or having them upset with you.

Since you are an Intuitor, you day-dream a lot and you sometimes drift off in thought and forget what you were doing.

Because of the NT combination, you love knowledge that is interesting to you just because it is knowledge. You worry about your competencies in all areas of life. You base your decisions in life on facts, information, and the logical outcome. To the Feelers of the world, your decisions may be considered inflexible, cold-hearted, and pushy. You have a strong need for fairness and for things happening the "Right" way. Because of this, you tend to worry about the problems of your family, friends, and acquaintances, thus becoming irritated and stressed out or making them irritated and stressed out. You also worry about what other people think about your ability.

Since you have an Intuitive mind that always questions, you probably continually question your own knowledge and competencies. You need people to express verbally their belief in your competencies, your correctness, and their support for you. You also need people to think and express that you are a knowledgeable person and that what you do is right.

You are driven to finish your projects or jobs whether you enjoy them or not. If you do not like a project anymore, you may need to decide that the project can be eliminated or finish it anyway, just so you don't have to worry about it. The J in your personality gives you the tendency to need to be on time and plan ahead. You basically have the attitude of doing things because they need to be done. Your feeling of pleasure comes more from finishing the project, than the act of doing the project.

Being this quiet, scientific, and finish oriented person, you will fit in almost anywhere if you don't get too pushy. You tend to be happiest in situations or occupations that involve problem solving, analysis, or a process dealing with knowledge or ideas, away from large groups of people.

When people do not meet your needs and expectations, you tend to downshift into anger. When downshifted you become very emotional (mostly hidden), with a more hawk-like behavior, just waiting for the problem to happen again. This emotion for the most part is not expressed immediately, but stuffed deep inside, only to be released when the last straw breaks the camel's back. The following giant outburst of anger will be surprising to the people present. They probably do not even know about all of the continual little things that accumulated to cause the outburst. When downshifted your personality will probably change to a more rule and regulation type of person, worrying about whether other people finish things or do things in the appropriate or correct way. When downshifted, with this rule oriented style, you might try to solve your problems through the process of making rules to control others. This might only lead to worsening the problems. People might say you have a chip on your shoulder when you are downshifted.

As with all temperaments, your natural qualities are needed in society. Your specific brain organization is found in, approximately, only 2.4% of the male population and .8% of the female population. Because of this, you probably have had a difficult time finding people who think and act like you do. Even though you might not admit it, growing up with few people to validate and support your beliefs and behaviors could have left you with an undeserved low self-esteem.

All in all, when happy, you are naturally a very valuable, quiet, problem solving, plan ahead, task completion, and scientific oriented type of person. Continue on page 49.

n. ENTJ

The ENTJ person is out-going and needs to be with people. When thinking you probably talk at the same time. Your world is the outer world of activities with people. You gain energy by being with people.

You have an inquisitive quick mind, able to see in and around situations or problems. You are able to come up with many possible answers to problems. Since you can see so many possible solutions, you may find it hard to accept authoritarian black or white type of answers. Being a T you are very good at arguing and debating. You could tend to express continually your disagreements with others, or to correct others. Doing this, you could end up being angry with others or having them angry with you.

Since you are an Intuitor, you daydream a lot, sometimes drifting off in thought and forget what you were doing.

Because of the NT combination, you love knowledge that is interesting to you, just because it is knowledge. You worry about your competencies in all areas of life, and base your decisions in life on facts, information, and the logical outcome. To the Feelers of the world, your decisions may be considered inflexible, cold-hearted, and pushy. You have a strong need for fairness and for things to happen in the "Right" way. Because of this, you tend to get involved in the problems of your family, friends, and acquaintances, thus becoming irritated and stressed out or causing them to be irritated and stressed out.

You also worry about what other people think about your ability. Since you have an Intuitive mind that always questions, you probably question your own knowledge and competencies continually. You need people to express verbally their belief in your competencies and their support for you. You also need people to think and express that you are a knowledgeable person and that what you do is correct.

You are driven to finish your projects or jobs whether you enjoy them or not. If you do not like a project anymore, you may need to decide that it can be eliminated, or you may finish it anyway, just so you don't have to worry about it. The J in your personality enables you to be on time and plan ahead. Basically your attitude is to do things the way you think they should be done. Your feeling of pleasure comes more from finishing the project, than the act of doing it.

Being this out going, scientific, and finish oriented person, you will fit in almost anywhere if you don't get too pushy. However, you are much happier in situations or occupations that involve problem solving, or analysis, dealing with people or knowledge.

When people do not meet your needs and expectations, you tend to downshift into anger. When downshifted you become very angry and argumentative (expressed both verbally and possibly physically), with a more hawk-like behavior, just waiting for the problem to happen again. When downshifted your personality probably changes to a more rule and regulation type of person, worrying about whether other people finish things in the appropriate and correct way. When downshifted, with this rule oriented style, you might try to solve your problems through the process of making rules to control others. This will only lead to worsening the problems. People might say you have a chip on your shoulder when you are downshifted.

As with all temperaments, your natural qualities are needed in society. Your specific brain organization is found in, approximately, only 7% of the male population and 2.4% of the female population. Because of this, you may have had a difficult time finding people who think and act like you do. Even though you might not admit it, growing up with few people to validate and support your beliefs and behaviors could have left you with an undeserved low self-esteem.

All in all, when happy, you are naturally a very valuable, out going, problem solving, plan ahead, task completion, and scientific oriented type of person. Continue on page 49.

o. INTP

The INTP person is a very private person. When thinking you are quiet and it may seem to others that you are in a different world. You gain energy by finding quiet times away from people.

You have an inquisitive quick mind, and you can see in and around situations or problems. You are able to come up with many possible answers to problems. Since you can see so many possible solutions to problems, you may find it hard to accept authoritarian black or white type of answers.

Being a T you are very good at arguing and debating. You may tend to express your disagreements to others continually or to correct others. Doing this, you could end up being continually angry with others or having them continually angry with you.

Since you are an Intuitor, you daydream a lot and sometimes drift off in thought and forget what you were doing. Because of the NT combination, you love knowledge that is of interest to you just because it is knowledge. You worry about your competencies in all areas of life. You base your decisions in life on facts, information, and the logical outcome. To the Feelers of the world, your decisions may be considered inflexible, cold-hearted, and pushy.

You have a strong need for fairness and for things happening the "Right" way. Because of this, you could tend to worry about the problems of your family, friends, and acquaintances, thus becoming irritated and stressed out or causing them to be irritated and stressed out.

You also worry about what other people think about your ability. Since you have an Intuitive mind that always questions, you probably continually question your own knowledge and competencies. You need people to express verbally their belief in your competence and their support for you. You also need people to think and express that you are a knowledgeable person and that what you do is correct.

You have little need or wish to finish the projects you like, since you enjoy them so much. If you do not like a project anymore, you probably will just eliminate it. The P in your personality gives you the ability to be spontaneous and flexible. Basically your attitude is to do things you like to do and only finish the other projects if the reward or pay is great enough.

Being this quiet, scientific, and activity oriented person, you will fit in almost anywhere if you don't get too pushy. Your biggest problem will be following through and finishing tasks. You tend to be happiest in situations or occupations that involve problem solving, analysis, or a process that deals with knowledge or ideas away from large groups of people.

When people do not meet your needs and expectations, you tend to downshift into anger. When downshifted you become very emotional (mostly hidden), with a more hawk-like behavior, just waiting for the problem to happen again. The emotion, for the most part is not expressed immediately, but stuffed deep inside, only to be released when the last straw breaks the camel's back. The following giant out-burst of anger will be surprising to the people present. They probably do not even know about all of the continual little things that accumu-lated to cause the outburst. When downshifted your personality proba-bly changes to a more freedom oriented type of person, worrying about being able to do what you want to do. People might say you have a chip on your shoulder when you are downshifted.

As with all temperaments, your natural qualities are needed in soci-ety. Your specific brain organization is found in, approximately, only 2.4% of the male population and .8% of the female population. Because of this, you probably have had a difficult time finding people who think and act like you do. Even though you might not admit it, growing up with few people to validate and support your beliefs and behaviors could have left you with an undeserved low self-esteem.

All in all, when happy, you are naturally a very valuable, quiet, problem solving, action, and scientific oriented person. Continue on page 49.

p. ENTP

The ENTP person is outgoing and needs to be with people. When thinking, you probably talk at the same time. Your world is the outer world of activities with people. You gain energy by being with people.

You have an inquisitive quick mind. You are able to see in and around situations or problems, and come up with many possible answers to problems. Since you can see so many possible solutions to problems, you may find it hard to accept authoritarian black or white type of answers.

Being a T you are very good at arguing and debating. You could have a tendency to express continually your disagreements with others or to correct others. Doing this, you could end up being continually angry with others or having them continually angry with you.

Since you are an Intuitor, you daydream a lot and sometimes drift off in thought and forget what you were doing.

Because of the NT combination, you love knowledge that is interesting to you just because it is knowledge. You worry about your competencies in all areas of life. You base your decisions in life on facts, information, and the logical outcome. To the Feelers of the world, your decisions may be considered inflexible, cold-hearted, and pushy.

You have a strong need for fairness and for things to happen the "Right" way. Because of this you could have a tendency to get involved in the problems of your family, friends, and acquaintances, thus becoming irritated and stressed out or making them irritated and stressed out. You also worry about what other people think about your ability.

Since you have an Intuitive mind that always questions, you probably continually question your own knowledge and competence. You need people to express verbally their belief in your competence and their support for you. You also need people to think and express that you are a knowledgeable person and that what you do is correct.

You have little need or wish to finish the projects you like, since you enjoy them so much. If you do not like a project anymore, you probably will just eliminate it. The P in your personality enables you to be spontaneous and flexible. Basically your attitude is to do things you like to do and only finish other projects if the reward or pay is great enough.

Being this out going, scientific, and activity oriented person, you will fit in almost anywhere if you don't get too pushy. Your biggest problem is following through and finishing tasks. You tend to be happiest in situations or occupations that involve problem solving, analysis, or a process dealing with people or knowledge.

When people do not meet your needs and expectations, you tend to downshift into anger. When downshifted you become very angry and argumentative (expressed both verbally and possibly physically), with a more hawk like behavior, just waiting for the problem to happen again. When downshifted your personality probably changes to a more freedom oriented type of person, worrying about being able to do what you want to do. People might say you have a chip on your shoulder when you are downshifted.

As with all temperaments, your natural qualities are needed in society. Your specific brain organization is found in approximately 7% of the male population and 2.4% of the female population. Because of this, you may have had a difficult time finding people who think and act like you do. Even though you might not admit it, growing up with few people to validate and support your beliefs and behaviors could have left you with an undeserved low self-esteem.

All in all, when happy, you are naturally a very valuable, out going, problem solving, action, and scientific oriented person. Continue on page 49.

CHAPTER 3
THE BRAIN FUNCTION DESCRIPTIONS

The following descriptions explain the cause and effects of each of the four Temperament letters that determined your Portrait. Each of your four letters has an opposite or secondary letter that was not chosen.

The descriptions below are those of a person with scores of 7,8, or 9 on either one of their chosen letters. If your score on either or both of your letters is 3,4,5 or 6 for any or all of the four functions, you may find that you have behaviors or characteristics belonging to both hemispheres for those functions.

Analysis

All four parts of the Sorter and each of your chosen letters are handled individually, and the cause and effects of the functioning of each hemisphere for all four major functions of the brain are covered.

The strength of your score determines your areas of brain usage. The closer your score is to 9 in column A, with the odd numbered boxes, the stronger the tendency is for you to do your processing for that function predominantly in the right hemisphere. If your score is closer to 9 in column B, with the even numbered boxes, your processing for that function is more often handled by the left hemisphere. Scores closer to 4 or 5 in either column mean that you probably use both hemispheres somewhat equally.

Please transfer the totals from boxes 1 and 2 on page 9 to the boxes below.

1. ☐   I

2. ☐   E

Part One: Thought Grounding

The results of this part of the Sorter involve the brain function of "Thought Grounding." These are the areas in the brain, right or left hemisphere, handling your thought processing.

If the score in box #1 is the highest, read under *Introversion* below. If the score in box #2 is the highest, read under *Extroversion* on page 51.

Introversion

The score in box #1 is the score that reveals your level of "Introversion" in the function of "Thought Grounding." Capital letter I is its common abbreviation. Only 25% of the general population are said to be Introverts. Although we all can have characteristics of both the introvert and the extrovert, if your score is closer to 9, Introversion and right hemisphere usage is more apparent. In the right hemisphere, the thought process is internal and nonverbal. This is because the right hemisphere is the visual, nonverbal, and the subconscious hemisphere.

Because of a spider web style of cell connection in the right hemisphere, the Introvert thinks in great depth, sorting through all areas of possibility. When thinking most, Introverts are quiet and tend to visualize their thoughts. Using the nonverbal hemisphere and not being interrupted by having to talk to others, things are thought through to a conclusion before being expressed. When the decision is completely made, the results of the thought process are transferred to the left hemisphere to be expressed verbally. Extroverts may react to this style of thought processing with great impatience, continually asking if you have an answer yet or maybe even if you are still in there.

Introverts prefer occupations away from too much contact with people. The act of being with large groups of people drains energy from high Introverts. If possible, Introverts would like to have periods of time to be by themselves to recharge their energy levels. Since Introverts only make up twenty five percent of the population, the continual pressure from Extroverts may leave Introverts feeling guilty about their natural way of thought processing.

The following is a brief review of the characteristics of a person who is right hemisphere dominant in the area of Thought Grounding.

Letter - I - Introvert - Right Hemisphere Dominant

Characteristics:

1. Subconscious hemisphere, lives in an inner world.
2. Communication halted, waiting for the conclusion of internal non-verbal processing.
3. Thinks inside quietly, visually.
4. Thought intense, in great depth.
5. Searching multidirectional thought.
6. Quiet even shy appearance since so much visualization and thought is occurring in a nonverbal hemisphere and is not communicated to those present.
7. Can be called selfish and made to feel guilty by others, since the Introvert's inner thoughts and feelings are not verbalized by the nonverbal right hemisphere.

Extroversion

The score in box #2 is the score that reveals your level of "Extroversion" in the function of "Thought Grounding." It is commonly abbreviated with the capital letter E. It is thought that about 75% of the population is Extroverted. The closer your score is to 9, the higher your level of extroversion will be.

In the left hemisphere the thought process is intense, into-the-moment, and usually verbal. This is because the left hemisphere is the conscious and verbal hemisphere. To think, most left hemisphere oriented people have a tendency to verbalize their thoughts. Most Extroverts will actually need to talk in order to think. Since thinking is "in progress" as they talk, they may give other people incorrect ideas about their final belief or meaning. This is because the Extrovert really hasn't made an actual decision yet. These misconceptions can cause anxiety on the part of both the Extrovert and the people listening.

Since their thought process is in the conscious left hemisphere, the intense into-the-moment hemisphere, high Extroverts can seem pushy and over powering to others, especially to Introverts. Extroverts with scores higher than seven may be unaware that they are invading other people's space and may not understand the source of anger or annoyance shown by people who want their privacy.

The sociable Extroverts are drawn towards people and people-oriented activities. Because of their need and desire to be involved, Extroverts may find it hard to concentrate in noisy active areas. Es may also find it very stressful if they have to be alone for long periods of time. Extroverts tend to like action and gain energy through interacting with other people.

Following is a brief review of the characteristics of a person who is left hemisphere dominant in the area of Thought Grounding.

Letter - E - Extrovert - Left Hemisphere Dominant

Characteristics:

1. Conscious hemisphere.
2. Communication verbal, auditory; Sociable.
3. Needs to talk when thinking.
4. Language structure and thoughts can be expressed in an incomplete form leading to misunderstandings.
5. Needs to experience surroundings, likes action, may act before thinking.
6. External, extensive, multiple relationships.
7. Gains energy from being with people.
8. Can be called over bearing or be seen as invasive into other people's space, especially the space of Introverts.

Part Two: Perceiving

Transfer the totals from boxes 3 and 4 on page 10 to the boxes below.

3. □   4. □
N   S

The results of this part of the Sorter involves the brain function that is normally referred to as "Perceiving." These are the areas of the brain, right or left hemisphere, where perception is handled.

If the score in box #3 is the highest, read under *Intuition* below. If the score in box #4 is the highest, read under *Sensing* on page 54.

Intuition

The score in box # 3 is the score that reveals your level of "Intuition" or right hemisphere usage for the function of "Perceiving." It is commonly abbreviated with the capital letter N. It is thought that only 25% of the general population are Intuitors. The closer your score is to 9, the more right hemisphere Intuitive tendencies you have.

The cell connecting structure of the right hemisphere is more like a parallel electrical circuit or a ladder. This cell processing structure can be more random like following alternate strands of a spider web or the up, down, or sideways direction you could trace on the picture of a ladder. This type of cell-connecting leads to a right hemisphere oriented more towards what is possible, rather than what is known. The spider web or ladder type of circuiting allows the neurons in this hemisphere to pass messages on in many directions, allowing a much faster processing for a larger input. This style of cell connecting allows a person to be more aware of a profuse quantity of sensory input, putting the Intuitor in a situation of seeing many possibilities and then questioning the quality of the present condition.

Since the input is directed to the subconscious right hemisphere, awareness of much of the stimuli is blunted and comes to the conscious left hemisphere in the form of a feelings or intuition. Many times solutions or answers to problems can seem to come to the Intuitor out of nowhere.

The Intuitive mind is a quick possibility-oriented mind. Intuitors seem able to see in and around a subject or problem, seeing all the variables and possible solutions. Seeing and questioning so much, Intuitors may have problems coming to conclusions until all the variables are covered.

An Intuitor may be fascinated with fantasy, fiction, the ingenious and imagination. Because of their right hemisphere perceiving, they may live for the future, looking to make things better, while at the same time seeming flighty, impractical, and unrealistic to others.

3   The Brain Function Descriptions

The following is a list of the characteristics of a person who is right hemisphere dominant in perceiving.

Letter - N - Intuitor - Right Hemisphere Dominant

Characteristics:

1. Sees patterns, relationships, has a sixth sense.
2. Senses interconnections, implications, sees the Big Picture.
3. Focused on the future, the present is a springboard, speculative, and innovative.
4. Sees estimations and approximations.
5. Possibility directed observation, lives in anticipation.
6. Can seem flighty, impractical, and unrealistic.
7. Need for reaction to input can be laid back in subconscious right hemisphere, unless downshifted and angry.

Sensing

The score in box #4 is the score that reveals your level of "Sensing" in the function of "Perceiving," commonly abbreviated with the capital letter S. It is thought that approximately 75% of the general population are Sensors. The closer your score is to 9, the stronger the use of your left hemisphere for Sensing will be.

In the area of perceiving, the left hemisphere's narrowed (compared to the right hemisphere) perceiving abilities are intense and immediate. This is because the information from the five senses goes directly to the conscious left hemisphere.

The left hemisphere has a neuron, or cell-connecting organization, that is different from the organization in the right hemisphere. Cells in the left hemisphere connect and pass on information in a linear pattern like a series electrical circuit. This type of cell processing or programing causes a goal-directed, linear, more narrow style of perception. This is because the left hemisphere is most often perceiving with an objective in mind. The series type of processing is slower, allowing in less sensory information. This causes the left hemisphere to ignore, or sometimes miss, sensory input that does not fit with its line of thought. The left hemisphere's intense and immediate handling of input also causes "Sensors" to be much more nervous about and reactive to what is happening in their environment keeping the Sensors in closer contact with their environment. People belonging to this group need to have and usually do have more control over their surroundings.

Since the left hemisphere of the Sensors does not question what it senses, the Sensors tend to accept and work with what is present in the here and now. This behavior makes the Sensors very practical and realistic. Since whatever the Sensor's left hemisphere sees is it, the Sensor relies greatly on facts and experience. Basically the Sensors are no-nonsense, down to earth, practical people who see the realities of situations.

The following is a list of some characteristics of a person who is left hemisphere dominant in perceiving:

Letter - S - Sensor - Left Hemisphere Dominant

Characteristics:

1. The five senses seeing specifics and facts.
2. Senses one thing at a time, concrete, in depth, yet narrow vision.
3. Focused in the present, practical.
4. Works with what is present in the here and now, sensible, remembers facts.
5. Strong need for control over their surroundings, staying in reality.
6. Goal directed observation, can miss some possible input.
7. Need for reaction to input intense with conscious left hemisphere.

Part Three: Evaluation

Transfer the totals from boxes 5 and 6 on page 11 to the boxes below.

The results of this portion of the Sorter involve the brain function commonly called "Evaluation." These are the areas in the right or left hemispheres of the brain where evaluation and decision making take place.

If the score in box #5 is the highest, read under *Feeling* below. If the score in box #6 is the highest, read under *Thinking* on page 57.

Feeling

The score in box #5 is the score that reveals your level of Feeling in the function of Evaluation. It is commonly abbreviated with the capital letter F. It is thought that 75% of females and only 25% of males are Feelers. The closer your score is to 9 the greater your use of or dependence on the right hemisphere for evaluation.

The right hemisphere, with its possibility, and parallel, ladder, or spider web-oriented processing, approaches making decisions in a random questioning comparative mode. The term Feeler refers to "Value Based Decision Making," not to the use of emotions. Association to past liked or disliked experiences and possible future liked or disliked results is common. People who evaluate by using the logical left hemisphere can find the decisions made by the associative random value based Feeler to be somewhat illogical, irritating, and unpredictable.

The evaluation process of the Feeler can take a longer period of time to arrive at a conclusion or can be extremely quick (I like it !). It is not unusual for the right hemisphere to fight the idea of making a decision because of many other factors available which could change the direction of the decision.

Because the right brain is the subconscious hemisphere, when decisions are finally made, they arrive in the conscious left brain in the form of feelings or intuitions, hunches or wants. This feeling or intuition is usually expressed as I-want-to-do-it-this-way, or I-would-like-this. When asked why such a decision has been made, an answer will be hard to find, since most of the evaluation process took place in the subconscious right hemisphere. If a demand is made by another person for you to explain the reason for your decision, you usually have to make up some kind of answer with your left hemisphere. After you answer, you will probably walk away, thinking that it wasn't the real reason, but "they" needed an answer.

Since decisions are based on the personal impact on all present at one individual moment, a decision made at another time, may change directions. This can seem illogical or wishy washy to others and cause much bewilderment. The Feeler is a people person both caring and emotional. They worry about other people and their problems. Feelers tend to be tactful, intimate, sympathetic, humane, and appreciative when not downshifted.

The following is a brief review of the characteristics of a person who is right hemisphere dominant in the area of evaluation.

Letter - F - Feeling - Right Hemisphere Dominant

Characteristics:

1. Comes to conclusions with an associative process using past likes and dislikes.
2. Concerned with interpersonal; what is the personal impact on all, present or not.
3. Decisions based on needs or impressions.
4. Concerned with past and future results of actions; good or bad.
5. Subconscious decision making, makes reasons for decisions hard to find.
6. Appears emotional, moods very obvious, whether expressed or not.
7. Concerned with extenuating circumstance, the humane, values, and intimacy.

Thinking

The score in box # 6 is the score that reveals your level of Thinking in the function of Evaluation. It is commonly abbreviated with the capital letter T. It is thought that approximately 75% of males and only 25% of females are Thinkers. This does not mean, that if you are not a Thinker, that you don't think. It only says that Feelers do not use their left hemisphere as often during the Evaluation Process. It also does not mean that if you are a Thinker you do not feel. It only says that Thinkers do not use their right hemisphere as often during the evaluation process. Thinkers in a downshifted mode move to the right hemisphere and can have strong emotions. The closer your score is to 9, the more you depend on your left hemisphere for the process of Evaluation.

The series, or loop style processing of the left hemisphere, causes a step by step, logical, cause and effect, and goal-directed evaluating process. Decisions are based on objective analysis based on facts and details. The left hemisphere's straight-arrow, cause and effect style of analysis does not leave any room for considering the impact on others in most situations. Not considering the impact on others makes this style of evaluation impersonal.

Because this method is in the conscious left hemisphere, Ts are much more aware of the evaluation process. Being conscious of the detailed evaluation process, Ts are very good at debating and arguing. Ts may miss some of the possible ramifications of their decisions because once the left hemisphere starts in a particular direction of thought, its cell processing structure makes it hard to take in opposing or non-relevant information.

Some of the decisions made by the left hemisphere can be looked upon as uncaring; the left hemisphere does not consider the impact on other people or even think that the impact is relevant. Thus people with left hemisphere dominance in evaluation are many times seen as inflexible and uncaring.

Ts are very involved in matters of fairness, justice, principles, and standards. Ts may be seen by Fs as distant, cold, heartless, and unemotional. However, this does not mean that Ts have no emotions, it just means that Ts may have a hard time accessing and expressing their emotions.

The following is a brief list of the characteristics of a person who is left hemisphere dominant in the area of evaluation.

Letter - T - Thinking - Left Hemisphere Dominant

Characteristics:

1. Comes to conclusions logically, using cause and effect.
2. Concerned with truth and right.
3. Decisions based on fairness.
4. Concerned with principles, standards, and evidence.
5. Needs consistency and validity.
6. May not consider the impact of decisions on others.
7. Can appear unconcerned, impersonal, cold-hearted, and unemotional.
8. Can be very effective at arguing or debating

Part Four: Primary Brain Orientation

Transfer the scores from boxes 7 and 8 on page 12 to the boxes below.

7. [____________]   8. [____________]

    P   J

The results of this part of the Sorter involves the brain function termed "Primary Brain Orientation," the area that determines what the awareness purpose for the brain is; what and why the brain will pay attention to input from the environment.

If the score in box #7 is the highest, read under *Perceiving* below.

If the score in box #8 is the highest, read under *Judging* on page 60.

Perceiving

The score in box #7 is the score that reveals the level of Perceiving or *Process Orientation* in the function of Primary Brain Orientation. It is commonly abbreviated with the capital letter P. Approximately 50% of the population is made up of Ps. The closer your score is to 9, the greater your use of the right hemisphere in the area of Primary Brain Orientation.

The right hemisphere Primary Brain Orientation function puts perceiving or gathering more input as the function of highest priority. The spider web or parallel wiring of the right hemisphere gives the Perceivers a continual desire to gather more information and experience more of their surroundings. To the questioning, inquisitive right hemisphere people, what they are perceiving is of foremost importance. Whether it's good or bad is of no significance so long as they enjoy what they are perceiving. Thus the P's lifestyle is activity oriented. They need to experience life and enjoy what they are doing.

The drive for completion of tasks is low because to finish a task you like means you can't do it anymore and you have to stop gathering information. There is little need to finish a task; it would end the Ps experiencing. Ps may be seen as indecisive and procrastinating. Ps will many times feel hurried and pressured by the finish oriented people.

The concentration on tasks that are liked is very high. Conversely, when tasks are not liked you can see people with high scores in this right hemisphere process getting off-task very easily. The joy for this group of people is the joy of doing or experiencing.

The following is a list characteristics of a person who is right hemisphere dominant in the area of Primary Brain Orientation.

Letter - P - Perceiving - Right Hemisphere Dominant

Characteristics:

1.   Senses for the joy of doing, to see and do what is enjoyable.
2.   Wants open-endedness, possibilities.
3.   Sees time in terms of opportunity to experience more, loses awareness of time.
4.   Tends to be spontaneous and random; If possible, Ps do what they like.
5.   Tend to postpone and handle tasks at the last minute.
6.   Scattered interest, can be indecisive if all possible activities are liked or disliked equally.
7.   May be called aimless and immature.
8.   May feel hurried and pressured by others, especially Js.

Judging

The score in box # 8 is the score that reveals your level of Judging or *Finish Orientation* in the function of Primary Brain Orientation. It is commonly abbreviated with the capital letter J and is thought to make up 50% of the population. This left hemisphere Primary Brain Orientation function puts evaluating, judging and closure as the highest priorities.

The linear wiring of the left hemisphere automatically leads to starting and continuing in a straight uninterrupted line to a swift conclusion. It is natural and necessary to continue a process to closure. To the linear wired left hemisphere oriented people, finishing, categorizing, organizing, and decision making are of foremost importance. They receive their joyful feelings from finishing a job or task. This need for and drive toward these feelings of joy or happiness could cause people of this hemisphere to have a preference to hurry or rush through tasks in order just to get them finished. Many times better solutions or decision may be overlooked. Js will continually have a high level of anxiety as long as they have tasks left unfinished. The larger the number of unfinished tasks the greater the anxiety.

The differences between peoples' Primary Brain Orientation function cause many problems in the areas of communication, understanding, and group cooperation. Js live by the work ethic, work comes before play. Since Js worry so much about completing tasks, they will be unhappy with any people around them who fail to complete tasks. This continuous worrying about task completion leaves the J with much tension and possible anger.

The following is a brief review of the characteristics of a person who is left hemisphere dominant in the area of Judging:

Letter - J - Judgmental - Left Hemisphere Dominant

Characteristics:

1. Looks for organization, an orderly, regulated, controlled life.
2. Wants to finish and get things done.
3. Needs punctuality, work before play.
4. Clarity, order, and structure must be pre-planned.
5. Anticipates and prepares.
6. A goal oriented and worrying mind.
7. Anxiety with self or others who do not prepare for or reach closure.
8. Can be seen as driving, pressuring, and inflexible to others.

These are the characteristics of each hemisphere for each of the four processes. These individual differences alone cause problems enough in communication, understanding, and meeting the needs of others.

Now let's see what happens when certain of the right or left areas' methods are combined together.

Chapter 4
THE FOUR MAJOR FACTIONS

With all of the different beliefs and philosophies that exist on this earth, it is surprising that there still seem to be just four major factions, groups, or types of people. The first report or description of the concept of four groups or factions was formulated about 2400 years ago, and the same concept has been reported and studied by researchers over the centuries ever since.

The types of people belonging to each of the four major factions share important beliefs, philosophies, and behaviors, helping previous researchers to identify them.

The quickest way of identifying who belongs to each group is by identifying which hemispheres of the brain each person uses for the different brain functions. Since you have already completed the Brain Hemisphere Usage Sorter, your specific group will be easy to identify.

The four groups are the results of special combinations of the right or left hemisphere Perceiving function with the right or left hemisphere functions of Evaluation or Primary Brain Orientation.

To determine which group or blend of groups you identify with, look at the scores in boxes 3 and 4 on page 10. If the score in box 3 is the highest, your right hemisphere dominates. You are called an Intuitor, abbreviated N. If the score in box 4 is the highest, your left hemisphere dominates for perceiving and you are called a Sensor, abbreviated S.

The Sensors have their highest score in box 4. For the Sensors to determine their groups, look at the scores in boxes 7 and 8 on page 12. If the score in box 8 is the highest, the J combines with the S to make a

SJ. If the score in box 7 is the highest, the P combines with the S to make a SP.

The Intuitors have their highest scores in box 3. For the Intuitors to determine their groups, look at the scores in boxes 5 and 6 on page 11.

If the score in box 5 is the highest, the F combines with the N to make a NF. If the score in box 6 is the highest, the T combines with the N to make a NT.

This is how the four major groups, the SJs, SPs, NFs, and the NTs are determined. The characteristic behavioral results of combining these specific hemispheres and their functions follows.

First, read your group's characteristics.

If you are an SJ read The SJ Combination below.

If you are an SP read The SP Combination on page 64.

If you are an NF read The NF Combination on page 66.

If you are an NT read The NT Combination on page 67.

The SJ Combination

When the left hemisphere Perceiving function (see Sensing on page 54) is in use with the left hemisphere Primary Brain Orientation function (see Judging on page 60), we have a person belonging to the SJ group. The SJ dominant individual combines the goal directed, into-the-moment, and intense Sensor Perceiving function with the time and finish oriented Primary Brain Orientation function. This combination of two functions, each of which are handled in the left hemisphere, creates individuals who have many special needs and behavioral characteristics in common.

SJs are locked in the here and now, with a need and drive for task completion, and thrive on manager and control positions. Organizing, setting up rules and procedures, and responsibility are the hallmarks of this group. Even though there are introverted and extroverted SJs and other SJs who make decisions using both the logical left hemisphere and the associative right hemisphere, all SJs tend to be locked in the present, driving towards organization and completion of tasks.

SJs receive many of their feelings of joy and happiness from seeing things go smoothly because of their organizational skills and from the act of completing tasks. Their world, with everyone and everything in it, is compared and judged according to the their view of how things should be.

Most SJs do not know that the non-SJs' view of the world and their role in it can be different or maybe completely opposite to the SJ's beliefs and philosophies. Because of this, many SJs live their lives with much anger and anxiety as they try to make other people into their own likeness. Some of what is normal behavior for each of the other three different groups can be and usually is looked upon by SJs as abnormal, disorganized, late, irresponsible behavior, which SJs need to correct.

When downshifted or angry the intensity of the SJ's reaction to and the awareness of what is happening in the immediate surroundings is heightened. This increase of awareness can be almost a hawk-like state where all attention is concentrated on the disliked situation.

SJs tend to strongly support the rules, laws, and procedures wherever they are. SJs enjoy being the stabilizers of our social and economic world, and also tend to create new rules and procedures when they feel things might get out of control.

A very high percentage of managers, principals, policemen, school bus drivers, administrators, book keepers, farmers, teachers, bankers, secretaries, clerks, accountants, federal executives, auditors and purchasing agents are SJs. They tend to work in society at occupations which complement their brain organization.

In other words, we tend to try to work at what we, as our brain, do well.

SJs depend on common sense and an intense ability to work with the reality of the here and now. If they find themselves in situations where creativity, spontaneity, dealing with the abstract, problem solving, and frequent change are most needed, they will probably be under a lot of stress. SJs can be found in all occupations, but they will definitely be happier in occupations, like those above, where the needed skills match the skills of the SJ.

The SP Combination

When the left hemisphere Perceiving function (see Sensing on page 54) is used with right hemisphere Primary Brain Orientation function (see Perceiving on page 59) we have a person belonging to the SP group. The SP dominant individual combines the goal directed, into-the-moment, and intense Sensor Perceiving function with the spontaneous, opportunistic, self-selecting process and perceiving oriented Primary Brain Orientation function. This combination of two functions, one of which is handled in the left hemisphere and one in the right hemisphere creates individuals who share many special needs and behavioral characteristics.

Being locked in the here and now with such a drive for self-selecting of their processes and activities, these individuals try to avoid or will act negatively in situations where strict controls or rules exist. Their into-the-moment and into-process combination creates individuals who have great concentration at tasks they like to do. Working with tools or at any activity they really like gives them the most enjoyment. Even though there are introverted and extroverted SPs and SPs who make decisions using both the logical left hemisphere and the associative right hemisphere, all SPs tend to be locked into the present, living a freedom oriented, self-directed, and, because of rebellion to rules, possibly a self-destructive style of life at times.

Their world and everything in it is evaluated and weighed according to the SPs' view of the value of the present processes and activities compared to their view of how life should be lived. Not knowing that the other three non-SP groups view the world and their role in it in a different or even completely opposite way, SPs can live their lives with much anger and anxiety. When downshifted, the SPs' level of anxiety and anger can be unusually high because of their desire for the freedom to do what they want to do when they want to do it. This problem can be very apparent in SP children living with strict inflexible parents. What can be looked upon as normal beliefs and behaviors by non-SPs can be looked upon by SPs as weird or ridiculous.

SPs tend to like situations where freedom of movement and freedom of choice are the rule rather than the exception. They also search for activities that fit their needs or talents so they can enjoy life. Since pleasure at the moment is such a driving force, SPs can be hedonistic and may often fail to plan for the future. SPs may leave, run away from, or quit when schools, families, marriages, and/or jobs get too controlling.

A high percentage of policemen, carpenters, farmers, sales people, cashiers, electricians, surveyors, cooks, typists, construction workers, dental assistants, marketing experts, plumbers, truck drivers, coal miners, steel workers, entertainers, paramedics, actors and actresses are SPs. In other words SPs try to work in occupations that combine freedom with activities that involve tools or processes. SPs depend on the combination of their ability to work intensely in the here and now with a strong innate drive to concentrate on, and perform tasks. Most of their activities or jobs deal with tools and machines or they may make use of their physical and artistic talents.

If they find themselves in an occupation missing these qualities or severely limiting their freedom, they will be under great stress and probably wish to quit. SPs can be found in all areas of our society, but definitely will be happier when they are in situations like those listed above.

The NF Combination

When the right hemisphere Perceiving function (see Intuition on page 53) is in use with the right hemisphere Evaluation function (see Feeling on page 56), we have a person belonging to the NF group. The NF dominant individual combines the future, possibility, all seeing, and laid back subconscious oriented Perceiving function with the associative, emotional, caring, and relationship oriented Evaluation function. When handled by the right hemisphere this combination of two functions creates individuals who have many special needs and behavioral characteristics in common.

Intuitors are aware of much more input from the environmental than the left hemisphere Perceivers. Combining this with the interpersonal, associative, possibility oriented evaluation method creates individuals who continually question who they are and what is their role and value in life. With an evaluative mode that depends so much on association to past experiences and future possibilities, NFs usually rely on likes, dislikes, goods and bads to make decisions.

Because the right hemisphere is so much faster at processing than the left hemisphere, NFs absorb a large amount of input into the subconscious right hemisphere, and because it is the subconscious hemisphere, there is low awareness of much of what is being seen or heard. Much of the reaction to the input is in the form of feelings or hunches about a situation. Because of this subconscious perceiving method, many NFs may seem laid back or unaware at times. However, when concentrating, they are aware of much more than the left hemisphere perceivers. NFs rely largely on nonverbal forms of communication in both giving and receiving.

Even though there are introverted and extroverted NFs and NFs that are both activity and completion oriented, all NFs tend to be locked into the questioning caring mode. Their world and everything in it is compared and judged according to the NFs' view of how things should be. Most NFs do not know that the non-NFs' view of the world and their role in it can be different or completely opposite to their own beliefs and philosophies. Thus NFs may live their lives with much anger and anxiety as they try to make other people into their own likeness. Much of what is deemed normal behavior by each of the other three groups could be looked upon as inflexible, uncaring, and narrow minded by NFs.

NFs spend a lot of their lives in activities aimed at helping others, while at the same time questioning their world and all of the ideas in it. A high percentage of counselors, fine artists, psychologists, journalists, teachers, clergy, social workers, writers, receptionists, actors, designers, musicians, composers, psychodramatists, librarians, architects, carpenters, reporters, editors, physical therapists, cooks, dental hygienists, surveyors, entertainers, optometrists and consultants are NFs. NFs have a strong tendency to work in occupations that complement their brain usage organization. NFs depend on their problem solving ability teamed with natural curiosity and caring to handle the situations and tasks in their lives. In situations where inflexibility, lack of caring, and anger are most common, they become extremely stressed. NFs can be found in all occupations, but they definitely are happier in occupations where the needed skills match the skills of the NF.

The NT Combination

When the right hemisphere Perceiving function (see Intuition on page 53) is in use with the left hemisphere Evaluation function (see Thinking on page 57) we have a person belonging to the NT group.

The NT dominant individual combines the future, possibility, all seeing, and laid back subconscious oriented Perceiving function with the logical, cause and effect, fairness, and consistency oriented Evaluation function. This combination of two functions, one handled by the right hemisphere and one by the left hemisphere, creates individuals who have many special talents, insights, behaviors and needs unique to them.

Intuitors are aware of much more input from the environment than the left hemisphere Perceivers. Combining this with a knowledge, factual and nonpersonal evaluation method, creates persons who continually question the how, what, when, and why of their surroundings. With an evaluative mode that depends so much on facts, information, and knowledge, NTs rely on observations, research or other factual input to make their decisions.

Since the right hemispherc is so much faster at processing than the left hemisphere, NTs take in a large amount of input to the subconscious right hemisphere. Since this is the subconscious hemisphere, the actual awareness of much of what is being seen or heard is low. Reaction to most of the input is largely in the form of feelings or hunches about the situation. Because of this subconscious perceiving method many NT may seem laid back or unaware at times. However, when concentrating, they will see much more than the left hemisphere Perceivers. NTs rely largely on nonverbal forms of communication both giving and receiving.

The combination of greater perception with the logical and analytical left hemisphere Evaluation function creates a person who has a clear insight into the how and why of the surroundings. This insight, which they feel everyone should have, causes the NT to get very frustrated with the incompetence of others. This can lead to problems on the job when an NT feels the boss or fellow workers are incompetent.

Even though there are introverted and extroverted NTs and NTs that are both activity and completion oriented, all NTs tend to be locked into a questioning and analyzing mode. Their world and everything in it is compared and judged according to the NTs' views of how things should be. Most NTs do not know that the non-NTs' view of the world and their role in it can be different or maybe completely opposite to their beliefs and philosophies. Therefore many NTs live their lives with much anger and anxiety as they try to make other people into their own likeness. Much of what is deemed normal behavior by each of the other three groups can be looked upon as inefficient, incompetent and/or incorrect by NTs.

NTs' lives are spent analyzing, solving problems, gaining knowledge and gaining competence. A high percentage of consultants, chemists, architects, attorneys, photographers, research analysts, judges, surveyors, chemical engineers, federal executives, biologists, psychiatrists, electrical engineers, principals, entertainers, designers, math teachers, research workers, actors, science teachers, marketing specialists, auditors, writers, dentists, psychologists, reporters, editors, fine artists, sales agents, journalists, accountants, musicians, farmers and contractors are NTs.

NTs have a strong tendency to work in occupations that complement their brain usage organization, depending on a problem solving ability teamed with natural curiosity and love of knowledge to handle situations and tasks in their lives. If they find themselves in a situation where there is inflexibility, incompetence, lack of efficiency and/or lack of knowledge, they will be under a lot of stress. NTs can be found in most occupations, but they will definitely be happier in occupations where the needed skills match their NT skills.

Chapter 5
THE BRAIN

Now, armed with your individual Profile, the descriptions of your individual Brain Hemisphere Functions, and the characteristic of your Major Group, it is time to see how the brain is structured and how it works to protect itself.

The human brain is a three pound mass that is each of us. The body with all of its miraculous parts is nothing more than a vehicle for us, the human brain.

We are who we are because of the portions of our brain we genetically prefer to use. If our brain is damaged, we may lose abilities or even change our personality. An injury to the brain and the following changes in the person's ability and behavior are clear evidence for how our abilities, attitudes, and behaviors are determined by the portions of our brain we normally prefer to use.

A man who has had a resent stroke approached me at a seminar. He had just listened to the information presented about the natural changes which can occur when the brain begins to rely on different portions of the different hemispheres. He seemed quite relieved that his new (and unusual to him) behaviors and feelings were a normal occurrence for his situation. It is important for people in these altered situations to understand the cause of their new found feelings, abilities and behaviors.

Imagine a brain that is unique only to you (unless you have an identical twin) and gives you your tendencies towards certain special talents and abilities; even though they are talents or abilities you might or might not fully develop, they are uniquely yours. Your distinct combination of aptitudes and talents are a special gift which only you have. To understand where this is leading and to understand what determines which special abilities you have or will have a tendency to develop, an understanding of some basic information about the structure and function of the human brain is needed.

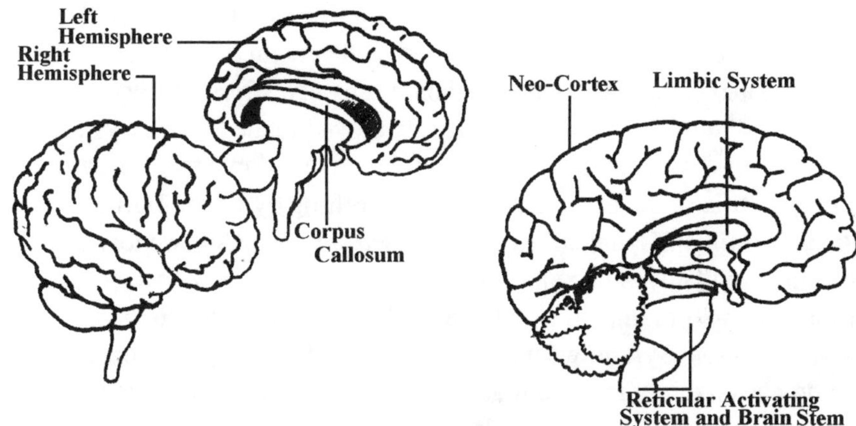

Illustration No. 1

Illustration No. 1 is a diagram of the entire human brain. The lowest portions of the brain, the Reticular Activating System and Brain Stem, control involuntary processes such as breathing, beating of the heart, etc. They also monitor and filter all incoming information and block out all unnecessary input. This includes everything from the unwanted sound of a ticking clock to the unwanted lecture on something we don't want to hear. This area is also sometimes described as the Fight or Flight, or *Reptilian Brain* since it is similar in structure to the entire brain of a Reptile. This is the fastest acting portion of the human brain and handles most periods of crisis, especially those having to do with life threatening situations; for example, when you are about to step off a curb to cross a busy street and out of the corner of your eye you see a fast approaching bus. The Reticular Activating System is what goes into action, and the result is that you may find yourself having jumped backward and landed on the ground trembling, with your heart beating rapidly. You usually wonder how you got there. This is because all the actions of this portion of the brain are subconscious. We do not usually remember what happened as we reacted in the actual moment of crisis. Apathy and disinterest, leading to low achievement and dropping out, can be traced to this portion of the brain. (The process for activating this portion of the brain and over-coming these problems is covered later.)

The middle portion of the entire brain is the second fastest-acting, the *Limbic System* often called the *Old Mammalian Brain* (Illustration No. 1, page 71). This is our emotional nurturing brain which handles sex drives, territorialism, needs for food, and general emotion and needs related situations. Anytime there is anxiety, stress, or anger we usually will move to or will have already moved to the Limbic System. As stated in "The Holistic View" (page 1) moving down to use a faster acting portion of the brain is called Downshifting by Leslie Hart in *Human Brain and Human Learning.* When we downshift we lose the direction, empathy, and control that is usually present when we are using our upper brain, the Neo-Cortex. When downshifted to the lower brain or Limbic System we might say or do things we would normally not do and so might regret our actions later. The lack of awareness of and control over the process of downshifting is one of the major causes of the many problems we have in our society. (This will be covered in greater depth in following sections.)

The *Neo-Cortex* (Illustration No. 1, page 71) is a slower but much more powerful portion of the brain. It gives humans an advantage over other animals, provided we can control downshifting. In *Fires of the Mind*, the portion of a video series entitled "The Infinite Voyage," when talking about the Neo-Cortex, it is stated:

> "For reasons still unclear to scientists, the brain in all mammals is divided into two hemispheres. Each is charged with controlling sight and movement on the opposite side of the body. In humans each hemisphere also seems to have developed very specialized duties. For most of us two separate speech centers in the left half of the brain enable us to speak and understand language. At the same time the brain's right half seems especially equipped to handle visual and spatial duties. A bundle of millions of nerve fibers joins the two halves of the brain and insures that they can instantly communicate."

Listed under Illustration No. 2 (below) are many of talents presently attributed to the right and left hemispheres of the Neo-Cortex. As we might expect the Neo-Cortex is a highly complicated and diverse area of the human brain explained later in greater depth.

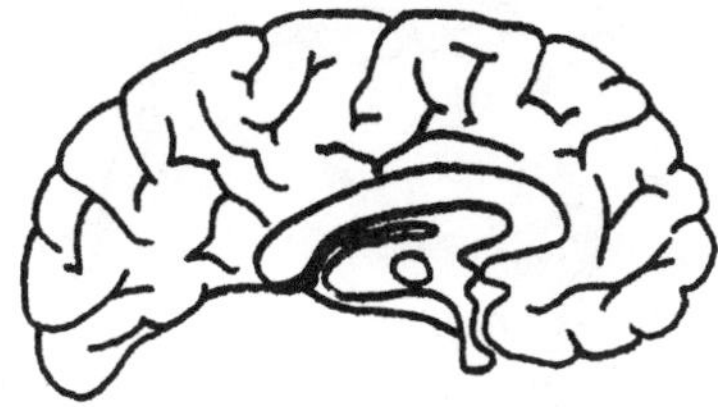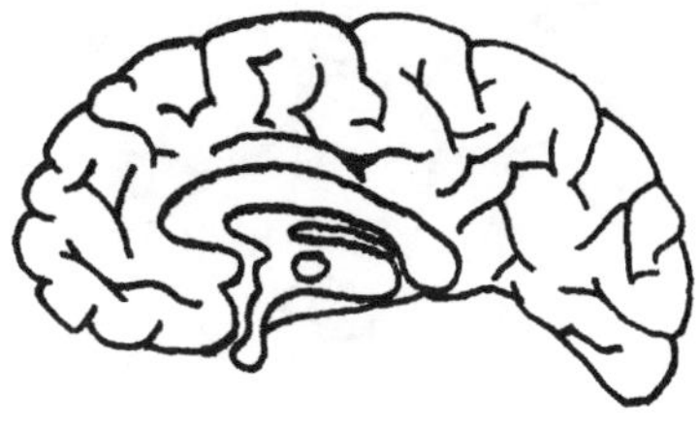

Left Hemisphere Characteristics	Right Hemisphere Characteristics
Analytical	Intuitive
Linear	Spontaneous
Sequential	Emotional
Concrete	Diffuse
Verbal	Nonverbal
Rational	Artistic
Explicit	Symbolic
Active	Playful
Goal-oriented	Holistic
Positive	Visual
Conscious	Subconscious
Ordered	Random
Efficient	Creative
Time Orientation	Event Orientation

Illustration No. 2

The nerve cell structure of the Neo-Cortex is where we find the cause, or source, of many of our individual talents and skills. In order to understand what determines which talents we have as individuals, we need to look at the structure and function of one of the approximately 100 billion nerve cells (neurons) that make up the largest part or portion of the human brain. In Illustration No. 3 (page 74) we see the basic structure of a nerve cell.

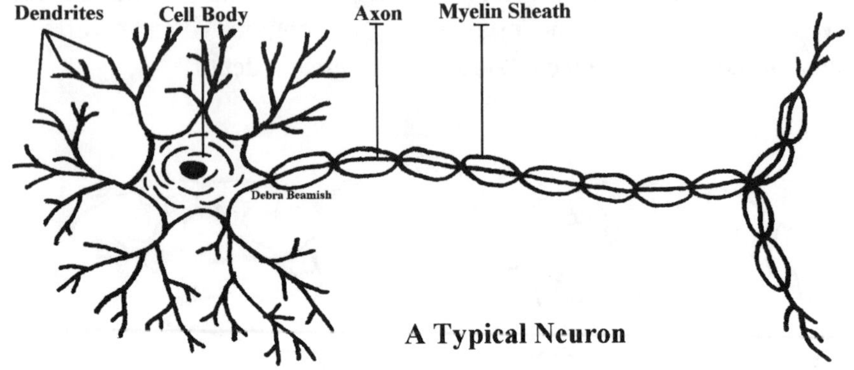

Illustration No. 3

A message is passed to the large end of the cell and if passed on, moves the full length of the Axon. When a message reaches the small end of the cell, it is passed on to the large end of another cell through one of the many Synapses or transfer points on one of the many Dendrite branches. It is estimated that each nerve cell, through its dendrites and synapses, can be connected to as many as 10,000 or more other nerve cells.

The method of connection from one nerve cell to another is shown in Illustration No. 4 (page 75).

The basic pattern of cell connection in the left hemisphere is different from the pattern of connection in the right hemisphere. The variety of differing cell connecting patterns is what gives the right and left hemispheres their unique and differing levels and types of abilities. (See Brain Function Descriptions page 49 for a description of the patterns and their effects.)

Until recently the dendrites have been one of the most overlooked and unexplained parts of the nerve cells. An important concept involving dendrites is that their presence in large or few numbers in specific areas of the brain determines our varying levels of knowledge and abilities. The development of larger numbers of dendrites per cell in each portion of the brain is how we gain greater abilities in each area of our knowledge, skills, and specific talents. Therefore we need to understand that in order to gain abilities or knowledge, we must study or

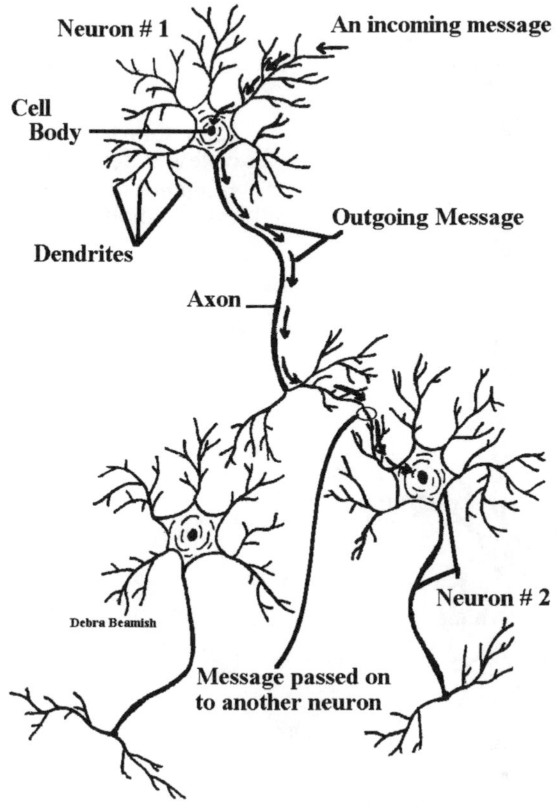

Illustration No. 4

practice a subject or an activity, causing the nerve cells in the correct areas of our brain to grow more dendrites and make more connections, thus giving us greater ability.

An excellent demonstration of this principle was recently presented by Dr. Arnold Scheibel in a video on the brain in a series called the "Infinite Voyage." Doctor Scheibel investigated the brains of a machinist and a salesman in the areas which control hand dexterity. By counting the number of dendritic connections on large numbers of nerve cells in the machinist's brain and also in the same area in the salesman's brain, Dr. Scheibel demonstrated that the nerve cells used for hand dexterity in the brain of the machinist had more dendritic connections than those of the salesman. An example of two neurons that have different numbers of dendrites is pictured in Illustration No. 5 below.

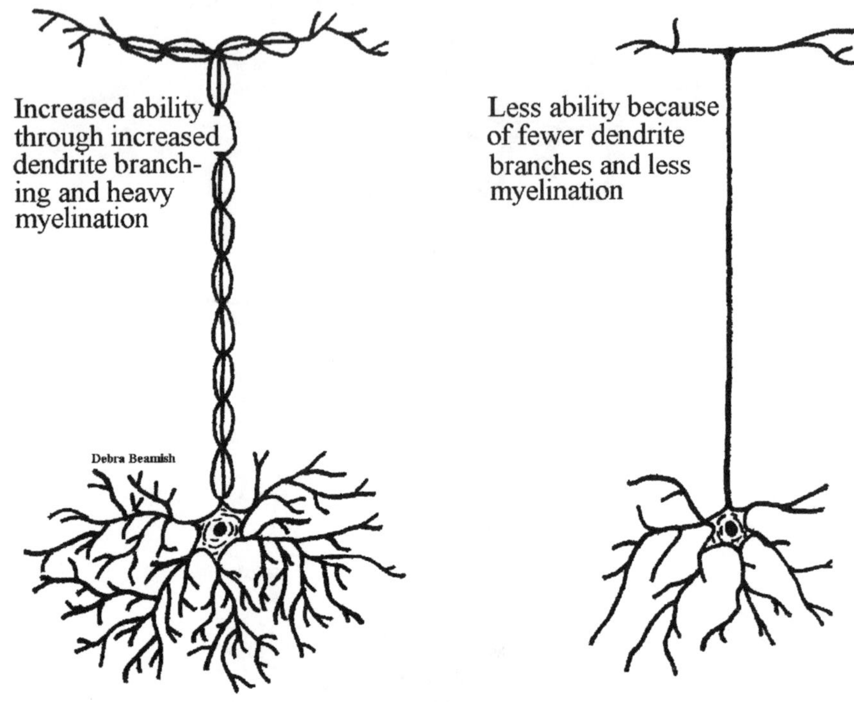

Illustration No. 5

In order to develop more dendrites you must use your brain. If you stop using a particular portion of the brain, the dendrites in that area will disconnect. In other words, we must use it or lose it.

The last important factor which dramatically affects the development of the efficient functioning of the brain is Myelination. Because the axon (see Illustration No. 3 (page 74)) carries an electrical charge, a white insulating layer of fat called Myelin is slowly deposited around specific axons throughout the brain. The areas which are myelinated and in what specific order they are myelinated is unique to each individual.

As myelination occurs in each section of the brain it increases the efficiency and ability of each specific area. The order of myelination in specific areas of each individual's brain and also the time schedule of when each area is myelinated are basically under genetic control. These differences in rate and area of myelination cause differences in ability between individuals. (The greater importance of these differences are discussed later.)

SUMMARY:

1. You are your brain; your body is simply a vehicle allowing you, as your brain, to move around.

2. We have looked at the four basic parts of the human brain.

    A. The left hemisphere of the Neo-Cortex is the logical, verbal, math, and vocabulary oriented hemisphere.

    B. The right hemisphere of the Neo-Cortex is the creative, nonverbal, art, and spatial oriented hemisphere.

    C. The Limbic or Old Mammalian System is the seat of basis natural drives and emotions. It is a faster-acting brain and where if not controlled, we downshift to, when we encounter stress. We cannot learn new information or have the control ability of the Neo-Cortex when we have downshifted to this portion of the brain.

    D. The Reptilian Brain or Reticular Activating System is the fastest-acting portion of the brain. This area is basically responsible for handling involuntary body processes, screening input, and is where we downshift to in cases of severe crisis or anger when we are ready to fight or react in order to survive.

3. The Growth of increased numbers of Dendrites in each specific portion of our brain determines which specific talents, knowledge, and abilities we attain.

4. The process of Myelination increases the functions of speed and clarity of the portion of the brain where nerve cells are being myelinated. Each person myelinates different areas of the different hemispheres at different times in their lives. In comparing children at home or at school these different rates and areas of myelination can cause children to be punished or labeled unintelligent just because their brain myelinates different areas than are needed to perform the given task, or myelinates the need areas at a slower rate than other children.

You now know how the brain functions and that we are all different on purpose with different needs and expectations. The next section reviews the basic needs and expectation of each of the four Major Groups. We can do this with a simple chart which shows what makes each Major Group either downshift or stay happy. Spend some time reviewing this chart so that you can see that the four Major Groups have some very opposite needs and expectations. The awareness of these, combined with the brain's tendency to downshift when needs and expectations are not met will be very important in understanding the problems and solutions to be presented.

Chapter 6
RELATIONSHIPS

Once we can see and accept that each person's behavior and belief systems are largely determined by their individual brain hemisphere usage pattern, we can start to be aware of how predictable behavior can be in relationships between people of different temperaments. Accepting the normalcy of other people's behavior and learning how to predict behaviors will allow us to gain tolerance in dealing with others and then more control over the success of those relationships.

The essence of what causes the anxiety and anger in our lives is the differences in the areas of expectations and needs between pairs or larger groups of people. Each person's individual brain organization has a specific set of needs and expectations that other people will or will not meet. First, we have to understand how an individual person's brain functions. Combine this with the concept that there are similarities between the people who belong to each of the four groups, and we can then begin to predict what needs and expectations most individuals within a specific group will have. For example, since the NFs continually question their value in relationships, NFs have a continual need to be repeatedly reminded of their value and importance in a relationship. Because of their own caring nature, NFs expect other people to act with caring and empathy toward them and toward other people. As with all other temperament groups, anytime the needs or expectations of an NF type person are not fulfilled you can expect anxiety or anger on the part of that person.

The following chart shows those activities and behaviors that generally either irritate or please the people who belong to each of the four major groups.

Temperaments Groups and Downshifting

Temperament Groups	What others do that causes this temperament to downshift or be irritated	What this temperament would like others to do to please them
SJ Left Hemi. Dominant	Don't follow rules Question authority Question procedure Don't finish tasks Bc late Be disrespectful	Be on time Follow rules Follow through with what you say Value their leadership Be respectful

SP
 	
Left with
Right Hemi.
	Give them orders
	Limit their freedom
	Question their values
	Hurt their friends
	Insist they do something
	  else
	Deny them the right to
	  believe differently
		Ask them for help
		Consider their point
		  of view
		Support their rights
		Be flexible
		Treat their friends
		  well
		Accept their right
		  to their beliefs

NF Right Hemi. Dominant	Yell at them Question their value Question their caring Not show you care Exhibit insensitivity Yell at others	Say you care Express their value Say they're needed Value their caring Recognize and appreciate differences in people

NT
 	
Right with
Left Hemi.
	Question their knowledge
	Question their veracity
	Make fun of their ability
	Argue illogically
	Talk down to them
	Create a commotion
	Be in authority
	  without competency
		Explain things well
		Value their thinking
		  ability
		Compliment their
		  abilities
		Accept their opinion
		Listen to them
		Agree with them

These problems of incompatibility and friction are similar to a chemistry experiment which was shown in a 7th grade science film. During a demonstration, a piece of sodium metal was dropped into a beaker of water. The sodium combined with the water giving off hydrogen gas. The heat of the reaction caused the hydrogen to ignite. The explosion broke the beaker throwing glass and water everywhere. This was a striking example of spontaneous combustion.

If you put two people together who have different needs and expectations you should expect some sort of friction leading to stress and anger similar to the spontaneous combustion above. Since genetically, approximately 75% of the time we are driven to marry a person who has an opposite brain organization, it is easy to see why there is so much stress in marriages and such a high rate of divorce. Oddly enough, yet predictably, even after a divorce a person guided by a genetically controlled selection process will usually again marry a person who has that same opposite brain organization, setting up the problems all over again.

The problem is we are attracted to a person of the opposite sex who has our opposite needs and expectation, yet for friends of our same sex we look for people who have a similar brain usage preference. Our close friends support our views, beliefs, needs, and expectations more than our spouse can or does. This can lead to bewilderment and anger at home.

When we add children, who have even different needs and expectations, to the stew we can have a very combustible mixture.

So are you lucky or not?

As a child, was your home life an explosive stew with anger and yelling or were you and your parents more compatible?

Remember: NO FAULT, NO BLAME.

The angers and frustrations or great family relations all happen without most parents even knowing the hows and whys of what is happening. Most people are honestly doing what they think is the right thing to do from their point of view.

Remember the upper brain, the Neo-Cortex, is the portion of our brain which allows us to control our behavior allowing us to think rationally, plan ahead, be empathetic, and control are emotions. When we see that a downshifted person is no longer using the Neo-Cortex or upper brain, we can see how downshifted members of a family, through anger and violence, can hurt other family members, causing increased anger and hurt throughout the family.

In most current literature these downshifted families are called "dysfunctional families." The ramifications of the results of these dysfunctional families show up in all areas throughout our entire society. Children naturally tend to copy their parents' behavior, so that the parents' anger and violence is perpetuated, appearing in our schools, businesses, and on into continuing generations within families.

The following chapter, Pitfalls and How to Avoid Downshifting, lists those actions that most commonly cause you to downshift into anger, according to your major group. By studying this section you may become aware of what actions or behaviors trigger your own downshifting as well as downshifting in others. With this awareness, couples can, if they wish, moderate their behavior in order to have happier lives. Just the awareness of why people act the way they do, and that their behavior is normal, will remove much anxiety from a relationship. Following each list of pitfalls for each of the four major groups is a strategy to help control downshifting. In the self-help section on page 133 you will find the pitfalls specific to children or students in school.

Chapter 7
PITFALLS AND HOW TO AVOID DOWNSHIFTING

First you need to know to which of the four major groups you belong.

If you do not remember your group check on page 62. The following descriptions should describe those things that commonly cause you to downshift into the anger or anxiety state.

Sometimes avoiding problems is easier than fixing them. Therefore, it can also be an advantage to know what causes your family and friends or fellow employees to downshift.

Remember, anger or downshifting usually occurs because of unmet needs and expectations combined with the idea that the other people involved are wrong or are just behaving that way to make you angry. If you read the other three sets of pitfalls, you will probably recognize things that you naturally do that make other people Downshift.

Read the pitfalls list first for your group only, then read the avoiding pitfalls section for your group only.

SJs on this page.

SPs on page 85.

NFs on page 87.

NTs on page 89.

Pitfalls of the SJ

May have anger towards people, who might question a rule or a set procedure, can push people away.

May have a strong belief that there is only one correct way of doing things, can be uncompromising, this can cause anger in other people.

May have a lack of flexibility which can lead to stagnation and lack of progress.

Preoccupation with rules as the correct tool to control other people's behavior can cause great conflicts with people of other temperaments.

Extreme need for closure can lead to a lack of awareness of possible better results.

May fail to act or participate because of a conflict with the procedures and/or philosophies of the organization or people involved.

Because of strength of convictions, people of this temperament who are in a position of power, can be over-demanding causing anger and subsequently decreased productivity.

With a tendency to have definite standards, people of this temperament can become biased against other people or groups of people who do not live up to their expectations.

May become quickly upset with those people who are unorganized, late, or those who have failed to finish a task.

Avoiding pitfalls

The SJ

In order to be their happiest and reach their greatest potential, SJs must accept who they are and learn how to control their brain.

Having the structure, planning, and detail ability that they do is the result of a left hemisphere dominant brain in the Perceiving function and left hemisphere dominant in the Primary Brain Orientation function. This is a brain which can organize, plan, and drive to completion when things need to be done.

The key to reaching your full potential and remaining happy is to value your own abilities and realize that most other people do not think as you do. SJs are estimated to make up only 38% of the total population.

People of other temperaments do not deal with the world in the same manner. They are usually unaware of how their behavior is possibly frustrating or downshifting the SJs. People in most cases just live their lives making decisions and acting as their particular brain organization determines is right.

Don't take decisions or actions different than yours as a threat to how you think the world should be run. Unless it is an illegal or life threatening situation, consider the rights of others to be different before you impose your rules or procedures.

Your close friends will think or feel as you do, but 62% of the people might disagree with your behavior. In fact, when we get married, almost 75% of the time we marry a person who has an opposite way of handling life's problems.

To avoid stress and anxiety, be selective and take a stand on only those situations that are most important to you.

In such situations, when you are starting to downshift, ask yourself these questions:

1. Are the actions or behaviors of the person involved something they are doing to you or just an inherited natural behavior?
2. If it is an inherited natural behavior, is it something the other person needs to be aware of and change or do you need to accept the person for who that person is?
3. Does the person involved know that what they have said or done has bothered you?
4. Does what they have said or done mean what you think it means? If you don't know, politely and in friendly manner ask the person what they meant.
5. Is what has happened important enough to worry about?
6. If the person meant to do or say what they did, is the person important enough in your life to be worth getting angry, upset, or hurt over?
7. If the person and the situation is that important, can you discuss the problem in a caring non-downshifted manner?

Remember, the SJ temperament is a valuable and needed temperament when happy and fulfilled. Relax and enjoy it.

Pitfalls of the SP

Preoccupation with freedom and the great drive to do what they what to do when they what to do it can cause conflict with people of other temperaments.

Anger in themselves or others can occur when parents, teachers, or bosses try to tell them what to do.

Leaving a home, a marriage, or a job can happen when conflict occurs during power struggles.

Behavior can be so spontaneous and negative that after a long cycle of rebellious behavior they might even question their own sanity.

Rebellious behavior and the accompanying rejection by parents or schools can put SP children in very dangerous situations.

SPs may fail to act or participate because of conflicts with rules or the demands of people or organizations.

May have friends like themselves because of a tendency to join groups of similar rebellious people to find support for and acceptance of their "socially labeled" negative behavior.

May have a sense of or an actual loss educationally, socially (family and friends), and financially when the desire for freedom causes them to leave or not to participate in a family, school, or job.

Avoiding pitfalls

The SP

In order to be their happiest and reach their greatest potential, SPs must accept who they are and learn how to control their brain.

SPs have the ability to concentrate on a task with the entire brain's ability. This is the result of a left hemisphere dominant brain in the Perceiving function and right hemisphere dominant in the Primary Brain Orientation function. This brain type can function with great clarity and attention when things need to be done.

The key to reaching your full potential and remaining happy is to value your own abilities and realize that most other people do not think as you do. SPs are estimated to make up only 38% of the total population.

People of other temperaments do not deal with the world in the same manner. They are usually unaware of how their behavior is possibly frustrating or downshifting the SPs. People in most cases just live their lives making decisions and acting the way their particular brain organization determines is right.

Don't take decisions or actions different from yours as a threat to how you think the world should be run. Because of your great desire to do what you want to do when you want to do it, you might find yourself downshifting (getting angry) so often that you are continually angry. Unless it is an illegal or life threatening situation, consider the rights of others to be different before you impose your will.

Your close friends will think or feel as you do, but 62% of the people might disagree with your behavior. Remember, when we get married, almost 75% of the time we marry a person who has an opposite way of handling life's problems.

Be selective and take a stand on only those situations that are most important to you.

In a situation that is important to you where you are starting to downshift, ask yourself these questions:

1. Are the actions or behaviors of the person involved something they are doing to you or just an inherited natural behavior?
2. If it is an inherited natural behavior, is it something the other person needs to be aware of and change or do you need to accept the person for who that person is?
3. Does the person involved know that you have been bothered by what has been said or done?
4. Does what they have said or done mean what you think it means? If you don't know, politely and in friendly manner ask the person what was meant.
5. Is what has happened important enough to worry about?
6. If the person meant to do or say what bothered you, is the person important enough in your life to be worth getting angry, upset, or hurt over?
7. If the person and the situation is that important, can you discuss the problem in a caring non-downshifted manner?

The SP temperament is a valuable, powerful, productive, and needed temperament when happy and fulfilled. Relax and enjoy it.

Pitfalls of the NF

May have low self-esteem from continual questioning of their own value.

May get angry or downshift because people do not care or because they think people do not care; may feel misunderstood.

May falsely attribute disliked behaviors or decisions of others to a lack of caring.

Can become over committed to helping others and taking on other people's problems.

For the ENFPs, anger in themselves and others can be caused by a questioning or disagreeing nature, no black or whites, only possibilities.

Because of continual self questioning, all NFs may lack a strong identity from which to base life's activities.

May attribute false motives to other people's behaviors or jump to negative or false conclusions.

May be taken advantage of or fail to act or participate because of fear of anger, yelling, or a fear of being rejected.

Preoccupation with being liked or disliked may cause decreased concentration leading to less achievement.

Avoiding pitfalls

The NF

In order to be their happiest and reach their greatest potential, NFs must accept who they are and learn how to control their brain.

To be able to care as they do is the result of a right hemisphere dominant brain in both the Perceiving function and the Evaluation function. Such brains naturally question, create, and associate in relationships with people and surroundings. It is natural for people of this temperament to worry about and question their standing in relationships with others.

The key to reaching your full potential and remaining happy is to value your own abilities and realize that most other people do not think as you do. NFs are estimated to make up only 12% of the total population.

People of other temperaments do not deal with the world in the same manner. They are usually unaware of how their behavior is possibly downshifting and hurting the NFs. People in most cases just live their lives making decisions and acting as their particular brain organization determines is right.

Don't take decisions or actions different than yours as a sign of lack of caring or even love. People can be in love and still see the world differently. Unless a situation is illegal or life threatening, consider the rights of others to be different before you question their caring or argue your point.

Your close friends will think or feel as you do, but 88% of all people might disagree with your beliefs and behaviors. In fact, when we get married almost 75% of the time we marry a person who has an opposite way of handling life's problems.

Beware of trying to help everyone and fixing everyone's problems. In order to avoid a lot of stress and anxiety, be selective and take a stand on only those situations that are most important to you.

In a situation that is important to you, where you are starting to downshift, ask yourself these questions:

1. Are the actions or behaviors of the person involved something being done specifically to you or just an inherited natural behavior?
2. If it is an inherited natural behavior, is it something the other person needs to be aware of and change or do you need to accept the person for who that person is?
3. Does the person involved know that what has been said or done has bothered you?
4. Does what they have said or done mean what you think it means? If you don't know, politely and in a friendly manner ask the person what was meant.
5. Is what has happened important enough to worry about?
6. If the person meant what was said or done, is the person important enough in your life to be worth getting angry, upset, or hurt over?
7. If the person and the situation is that important, can you discuss the problem in a caring non-downshifted manner?

The NF temperament is a beautiful, valuable and needed temperament when happy and fulfilled. Relax and enjoy it.

Pitfalls of the NT

May cause negative feelings in others with an overpowering attitude: I'm right, do it my way.

Preoccupation with and the extreme belief in the correctness of their own ideas and knowledge to the exclusion of and the correcting of others can cause great conflict with members of their own and other temperaments.

May attribute false motives to people's behaviors or ideas and may jump to negative or false conclusions.

May have a strong tendency to doubt their own abilities (introverts) and the abilities of other people. This includes the tendency to continually check and recheck to make sure that things are done "correctly."

Anger at incompetence and stupidity of others or anger at themselves if they make mistakes, may lead them to isolating themselves from other people and/or quitting an activity.

Anger in themselves and others may be caused by a disagreeing, arguing, or questioning nature.

May fail to act or participate because of a fear of showing a lack of knowledge or ability.

Can be disrespectful to people found lacking, including superiors. Because of their possible arrogance, NTs may ignore rules found unjustified.

May fail to act or participate because of a belief that the people involved are incompetent.

Avoiding pitfalls

The NT

In order to be their happiest and reach their greatest potential, NTs must accept who they are and learn how to control their brain.

The insight that they have is the result of a brain which is right hemisphere dominant in the Perceiving function and left hemisphere dominant in the Evaluation function. This is a brain which can see in and around situations, understanding or wanting to understand how things work or what things mean.

The key to reaching your full potential and remaining happy is to value your own abilities and realize that most other people do not think as you do. NTs are estimated to make up only 12% of the total population.

People of other temperaments do not deal with the world in the same manner. They are usually unaware of how their behavior is possibly frustrating or downshifting the NTs. People in most cases just live their lives making decisions and acting as their particular brain organization determines is right.

Don't take decisions or actions different from yours as a threat to the value of your intelligence, competency or as a situation where your knowledge is immediately needed as a correcting force. Unless it is an illegal or life threatening situation, consider the rights of others to be different before you impose your beliefs, knowledge, or controls.

Your close friends will think or feel as you do, but 88% of the people might disagree with your beliefs and behaviors. In fact, almost 75% of the time we marry a person who has an opposite way of handling life's problems.

Beware of a repetitive cycle of correcting others, being rejected, downshifting, becoming negative and over sensitive, etc. This can lead to a power struggle which can only lead to isolation.

Beware of trying to correct everyone and fixing everyone's problems. In order to avoid a lot of stress and anxiety, be selective and take a stand on only those situations that are most important to you.

In a situation that is important to you where you are starting to downshift, ask yourself these questions:
1. Are the actions or behaviors of the person involved something that the person is doing to you or just an inherited natural behavior?
2. If it is an inherited natural behavior, is it something the other person needs to be aware of and change or do you need to accept the person for who that person is?
3. Does the person involved know that what was said or done has bothered you?
4. Does what they have said or done mean what you think it means? If you don't know, politely and in a friendly manner ask the person what was meant.
5. Is what has happened important enough to worry about?
6. If the person meant what was said or done, is the person important enough in your life to be worth getting angry, upset, or hurt over?
7. If the person and the situation is that important, can you discuss the problem in a caring non-downshifted manner?

Remember, the NT temperament is an insightful, powerful, positive, and needed temperament when happy and fulfilled. Relax and enjoy it.

Read on for an understanding of how all of this lack of knowledge and misunderstanding affects different areas of our society.

Chapter 8
HOME, FAMILY, AND FRIENDS AND ENEMIES: THE PROBLEM

Male to male and female to female, we, as our genetically designed brain, search for a friend or group of friends to validate our beliefs and philosophies, and praise our abilities. The need for praise and validation is an integral and crucial need of the human brain. This validation or lack of validation gives us either the strength of high self-esteem, or possibly the fears and lack of confidence of low self-esteem. Both situations put us in a position where we can help or hurt other people, but in different ways and degrees. Strength of will could allow us to be tolerant, accepting and supporting or, when downshifted, domineering, controlling and degrading. Low self-esteem leaves a person with less strength to be supporting towards others and a quickened tendency to downshift to anger, leading to a domineering, controlling and degrading nature.

When we marry, because of differences in structure between the male and the female brain and also because of a genetic induced preference for mixing the gene pool, we quite often marry a person who has an opposite brain hemispheric usage pattern. The differences between spouses can be complementary and positive, but most often the differences in behavior, thinking method, beliefs, needs, expectations, and philosophies can soon cause irritation and anger. Since the parents of different temperament have different genetics to give to their children, some of the children will have a tendency to have different abilities and different belief systems than either one or maybe both of their parents.

These differences also tend to cause problems within the home.

Remember, "No Fault, No Blame." Most people do what they think is right for other people not knowing, not accepting, or possibly even not caring that they are downshifting and hurting the others. A common statement or belief is:

> "It is my duty and responsibility to make you do what is good for you."

The problem with this statement or belief is, if the other person has a different brain hemispheric usage pattern than the controlling parent, spouse, boss, friend, etc., the person being told what to do might not agree with what you feel is right.

These disagreements lead to possible confrontation with anger and downshifting by both individuals involved. In the name of misplaced self righteousness we can drive children from our homes and schools, spouses from marriages, and employees from their jobs. The sad part about this is that it can happen over little things that are not really important to the success, failure or safety of the people involved. The continual validation of the controller by a selected group of friends who have the same brain caused beliefs, philosophies, and behaviors can make the problem even worse, causing the person to be even more self-righteous and less tolerant or accepting of differences.

Even if the people do not leave, there are still negative results from this over-controlling, molding behavior. Normally, in situations of dis-agreement leading to downshifting, both happiness and achievement will decrease with those involved. The achievement results of happy and unhappy students (Chapters 9, page 102) are good examples of this problem's results.

So the people involved are unknowingly decreasing self-esteem and achievement throughout society. This happens as we attempt, with good intentions, to create people in our own image by trying to make them think and do things in the way that we "think" is right. At the same time, by not valuing and praising their different unique abilities and beliefs, we also help decrease self-esteem and their future productivity.

Based on the four basic factions in our society and how they inter-act (page 80), it is easy to see how natural and predictable these negative interactions are. The key to lessening the problems is to educate the public so that there is more tolerance, support, and acceptance of individual differences. A well-integrated program at the topmost level must be implemented to remedy the problem. Only a program of this scale can increase happiness, self-esteem, and productivity for all concerned.

Chapter 9
SCHOOLS: THE PROBLEM

Once while asking a colleague for suggestions for the name of this book, the following, which ably describe the problem, were suggested:

Unintentional Social Discrimination in our Schools
Is Social Discrimination Frustrating Young Minds
Eliminating Social Discrimination in our Schools
How Damaging is Social Discrimination in our Schools
Social Discrimination and the Nonconforming Student
The Far Reaching Affects of Social Discrimination in our Schools
Social Discrimination—The Accepted Abuse of Young Minds
Social Discrimination—An Unnecessary Shortcoming in our
    Schools
Social Discrimination—An Obstacle to Learning

These suggestions brought the problem into a new light. Look at the key ideas; Obstacle to learning. Unnecessary. Abuse of young minds. Far reaching affects. Nonconforming students. Unintentional. Damaging. Frustrating. Eliminate. Each of these words or phrases describes one facet of the problem. But just the concept of discrimination, even though it seems like such a derided or negative word, describes the entire situation very well.

We take students of varying brain hemisphere usage preferences and treat them as if they all had the same needs, expectations, talents, and abilities. Each teacher, because of his or her individual temperament, has a different set of needs and expectations. If the abilities and behaviors of a particular student in a class do not match up to the individual teacher's needs and expectations, the student will be graded down or possible repeatedly disciplined. Students have no control over the teachers they will have; therefore, sometimes they will be lucky and match up and sometimes they won't. Some students, who have inherited brain organizations that just do not fit well in school, may only find one or two teachers with whom they can get along. Students have no control or choice over which areas of their brain are genetically determined to myelinate and develop their special aptitudes, needs, and expectations. The act of continuous negative evaluation of their deficits or behaviors is indeed a form of social discrimination.

Presented in many college classes is a parable called " A Fable for Learners;" lacking an author's credit, it is quoted here as "author unknown." The fable describes the situation extremely well.

A Fable for Learners

One time the animals had a school. The curriculum consisted of running, climbing, flying, and swimming, and all the animals took all the subjects.

The duck was good in swimming, better in fact than his instructor, and he made passing grades in flying, but he was practically hopeless in running. Because he was low in this subject he was made to stay in after school and drop his swimming class in order to practice running. He kept this up until he was only average in swimming. But average is acceptable, so nobody worried except the duck.

The rabbit started out at the top of the class in running but he had a nervous breakdown and had to drop out of school on account of so much make-up work in swimming.

The squirrel led the climbing class, but his flying teacher

made him start his flying lesson from the ground up instead of from the top of the tree down. He developed charley horses from over-exertion at the take-off, and began getting Cs in climbing and Ds in running.

The practical prairie dog apprenticed their offspring to a badger when the school authorities refused to add digging to the curriculum.

At the end of the year, an abnormal eel, that could swim fairly well, climb and fly a little, was made valedictorian.

(Author Unknown)

This fable points out how animals have natural differences in abilities, needed in order to allow the animals to live successfully and survive in varying environments. When we imagine them in a school system, their environmentally needed differences became a hindrance in competing in the rigid school and curriculum setting.

Each school, depending upon the brain hemispheric usage patterns of the school board, principals, teachers, and parents has certain needs and expectations of the students. The students, like the animals in the fable, have special differences in ability, aptitudes, behaviors, needs, and expectations all of which are necessary so they can fulfill their role in society. The differences between the school's needs and expectations and the individual student's capabilities and behaviors frequently leads to negative situations.

The original question was: "Why do different students achieve at different levels in different classes?" Four main reasons for student low achievement are apparent.

First, is the area of the student's abilities and aptitudes not matching up with the needs of the particular class. Both the curriculum and the teacher's specific requirements enter the mix. Imagine you are a boy who has not myelinated the areas in the brain which produce good hand-eye coordination in a class where all work is graded on neatness. No matter how hard you try and how good your thoughts are your grades are always low because of your hand writing and lack of neatness. Then ask yourself, how would I feel if I were put into this situation?

Depending upon which areas of our brain are myelinated or not myelinated we have special aptitudes and areas of weakness. To continually grade students negatively downward in areas of weakness, not only causes low self-esteem, but also, through downshifting, negatively affects their levels of achievement in areas where they have strong abilities.

The second reason for a student's poor achievement is caused by the brain's natural act of downshifting in order to handle situations involving anxiety. We all experience periods of stress and anger in our homes, on the job, and in many of life's difficult situations. The idea examined now will be how this anger affects our degree of happiness and how our degree of happiness affects our levels of achievement. Most people would agree when you are angry with your boss at work or your family at home your desire to work your hardest is decreased.

Working with 6th, 7th, and 8th grade science students, an intriguing question was: What caused the students to achieve at such differing levels? One student would achieve As in one class, but would get low grades in other classes. Other students would receive low grades in classes, when they seemed to be very intelligent. These incongruities started this teacher looking about for the reasons why otherwise capable students either refused to or were unable to achieve at higher levels.

The first thing the students were tested on was their level of auditory, visual, and kinesthetic sensory awareness. All the results from all sources were recorded on an oversized seating chart so visual comparisons could be made. Their scores on Metropolitan Achievement Test were compared to their level of success in the classroom. At this stage of the research, the Keirsey Temperament Sorter from the book, *"Please Understand Me"* by Dr. David Keirsey was used, with his permission, to test the students. Later the Brain Hemisphere Usage Sorter was designed and used. All of the students were tested and the results were added to the chart in order to continue searching for some correlation to their differing levels of success.

Two years were spent in a fruitless search for a correlation to provide an answer to the original question: Why do different students achieve at different levels in different classes? More information was needed. Looking over the classroom it seemed the next step must be to ask the students some questions to get more information, then compare the new information with their levels of achievement. The rapport with the students was good; they had been in my classroom for three years, so truthful answers could be expected. The students were given five choices for answers. They were "yes," "yes yes," "no," and "no no," and "no answer." In case they did not remember or they felt the information was too personal and didn't want to answer, they were given the choice of a "no answer" response. The following is a list of the questions used:

1.   Did your parents stimulate you by reading to you, putting a mobile above your crib or bed, or by playing music for you from birth through preschool?
2.   Do your parents expcct you to do well in school?
3.   How many teachers have you liked up through this grade?
4.   Did you actually work hard on the Metropolitan Achievement Test?
5.   Have you found the school system to be fair? Are you happy at school?
6.   Do you have a happy home life?
7.   How many times have you changed schools?

The students recorded their answers on their own paper, putting their name at the top. Their answers for the most part were very explicit. Some students even put down the different years when they were happy or unhappy and what happened in their lives to cause the changes.

The answers were compared and graphed with the student's grade averages in school. The two questions which finally pointed to a possible cause for the student's inconsistent achievement were questions 5 and 6. There was a high correlation between unhappiness and low achievement and happiness and high achievement. Chart #1 (page 102) shows the results.

Looking at the left hand section of the four sections of Chart #1, we can see that approximately 81.8% of the students who reported that they were happy at home and happy at school achieved a building wide grade average of 3.0 or better. When we look at the achievement of those students who said they were happy at school but unhappy at home we still find 76% of the students achieving with a 3.0 or better grade average building wide. It is not until we look at the achievement of those students who reported being unhappy at school and happy at home that we see a drop in achievement so that only 50% of the students have a 3.0 or better grade average. When we look at the last group of students we see that only 20% of the students who report being unhappy at school and unhappy at home can maintain a 3.0 or better grade average.

The most crucial factor that affects the students' achievement rate in school is whether or not they are happy or unhappy at school. Depending upon how well the special needs and expectations of the teacher match those of the student, students will either stay in their upper Neo-Cortex or downshift to the lower Limbic System or even further down to the Reticular Activating System. The act of downshifting or moving into the Limbic System within the brain, in order to handle situations causing anxiety, creates a situation where students can not or will not learn.

As stated in the Holistic View:

This inability or lack of desire to accept, listen to, or like the people of differing brain hemispheric usage preferences is further complicated by the process called downshifting which is described in Leslie Hart's book, *Human Brain and Human Learning*. In his book, Hart states:

"When the individual detects threat in an immediate situation, full use of the great new cerebral brain is suspended, and faster-acting, simpler brain resources take larger roles."

When students have that feeling of anxiety, anger, fear, etc. they have "Downshifted" and they are using an older portion of their brain called the *Old Mammal Brain* or Limbic System. It usually starts with what I describe as the "Repeating Tape" which is when their brain starts silently or they start verbally saying over and over such things as: That isn't fair..They/you can't make me do it..They have no right to..I don't have to..I don't like this ..Why me?..I won't! At this point they are at level one of Downshifting. The student does not listen to what the teacher says, they can not learn, and they may make many self- destructive decisions that they would not normally make if they were not "Downshifted."

Since students who are not using their Neo-Cortex cannot learn, anything that causes them to downshift causes decreased achievement.

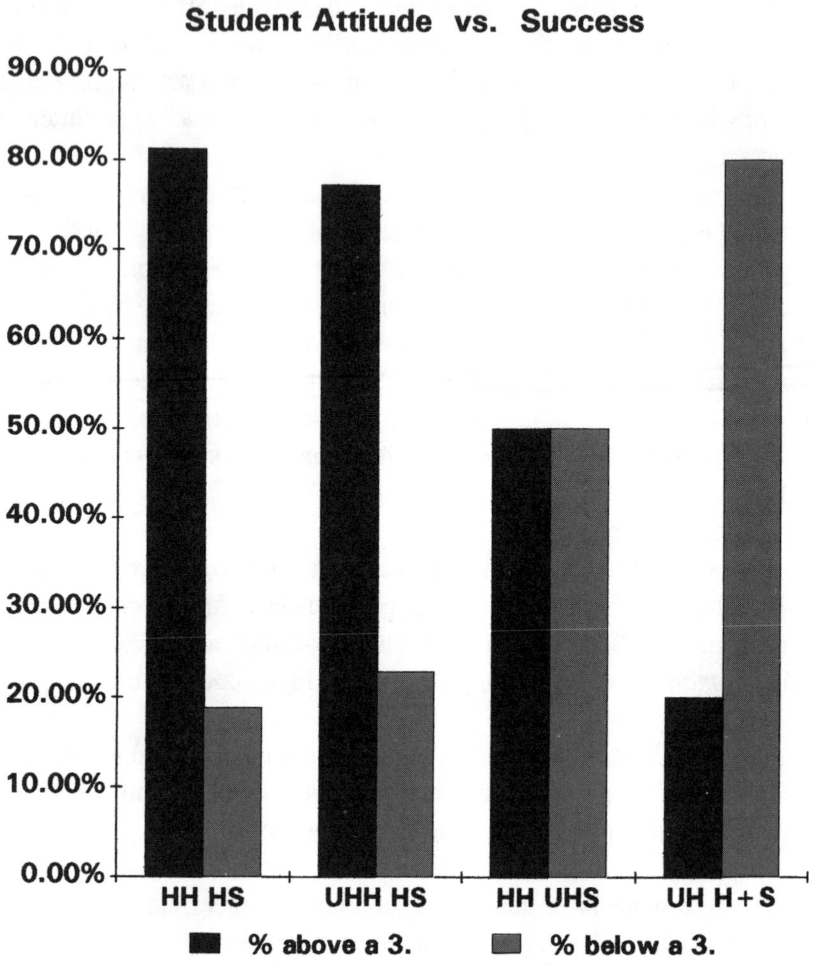

Chart No. 1

This concept of downshifting allows us to understand why a great many students can spend so much time in our schools and learn so little. We must realize that when individual brain hemisphere usage tendencies differ between teachers and students, some students will feel anxiety and downshift. This downshifting in the student's brain causes the student to lose the ability to learn until the threat is removed or the problem solved. In many situations, certain students, disliking a subject or a teacher, will downshift to an angry state where their ability to learn is effectively nonexistent. These same students, in a different situation with a different teacher or subject, will no longer be in a downshifted mode and will get an A from this class. Remember, when comparing the level of achievement with whether a student is happy or unhappy on the graph above, we saw how important it was for us to realize that the way we treat students, affects their level of achievement.

During the research all the students were tested for brain hemisphere usage patterns, and surveyed as to their level of happiness at home and school. Chart #2 (page 104-105) shows the differences in levels of achievement for all the 16 temperament groups. These differences are graphically apparent.

By studying this chart we can see that each major temperament group with its particular needs and expectations reacts differently to the educational system. Different things will cause each group to downshift at different times according to how they are treated by a specific teacher. This periodic downshifting, as students and teachers of differing temperament meet and interact, causes an inability to learn. The inability to learn causes low achievement and low self-esteem for students and stress and anxiety for teachers. The low achievement, low self-esteem, and continual anger causes many students to drop out of school, 28.6% nationally. The stress and anxiety also leads to early burnout for many teachers.

The third problem area is largely a societal problem. We have developed an apathetic student body in many of our schools. Probably the most neglected and misunderstood portion of the brain is the Reticular-Activating System (R.A.S.), the lowest portion of the brain including the brain stem. The R.A.S. portion of the brain is where decisions are made about the importance of incoming sensor input: In other words, whether a person will pay attention to what is happening in the surrounding environment. It is glaringly clear to those who see the problem, that there is no organized attempt by the educational system, the media, nor society as a whole to instill in the minds of students a belief in the value and necessity of an education. Consequently we have created a highly apathetic, fun-loving, inattentive student body. Our students' achievement levels vary according to interest in subject, entertainment level of the presentation, and the likability level of the teachers involved.

It is no wonder that achievement levels and drop-out levels within

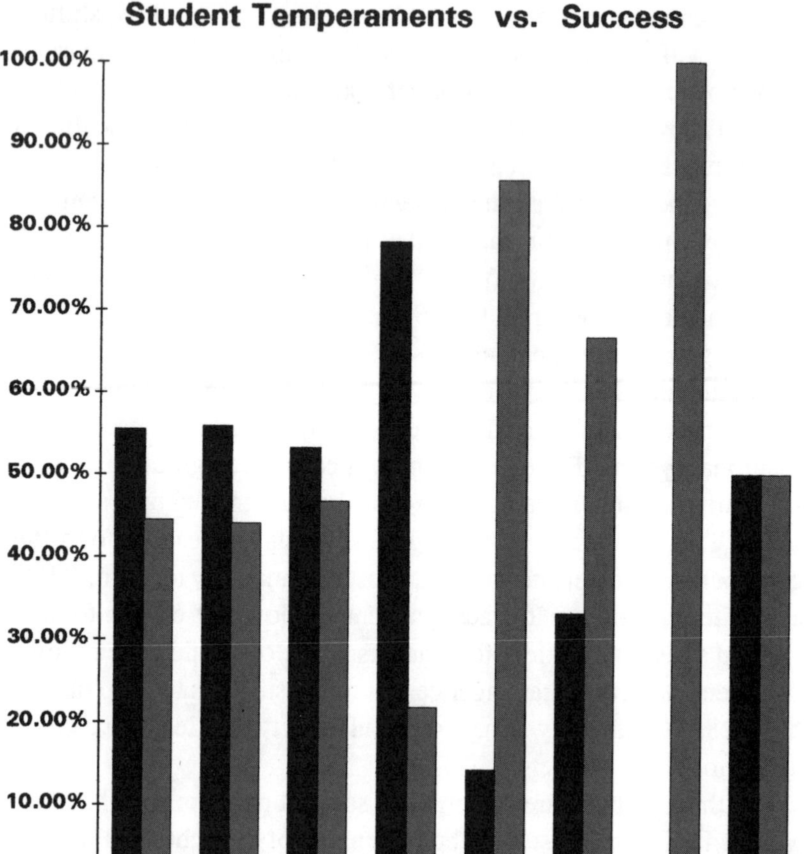

Chart No. 2

our schools are not where we want them. The media, the parents, and the schools have failed to develop in the students a respect and desire for an education. If students do not feel a class is important, the chances are that they will not pay attention or work very hard on the material.

The last main factor is a lack of ability to discipline students or make them pay attention. For hundreds of years, strong family expectations and fear of corporal punishment kept the R.A.S. portions of the students' brains attentive to the educational process. In today's public

Chart No. 2 continued.

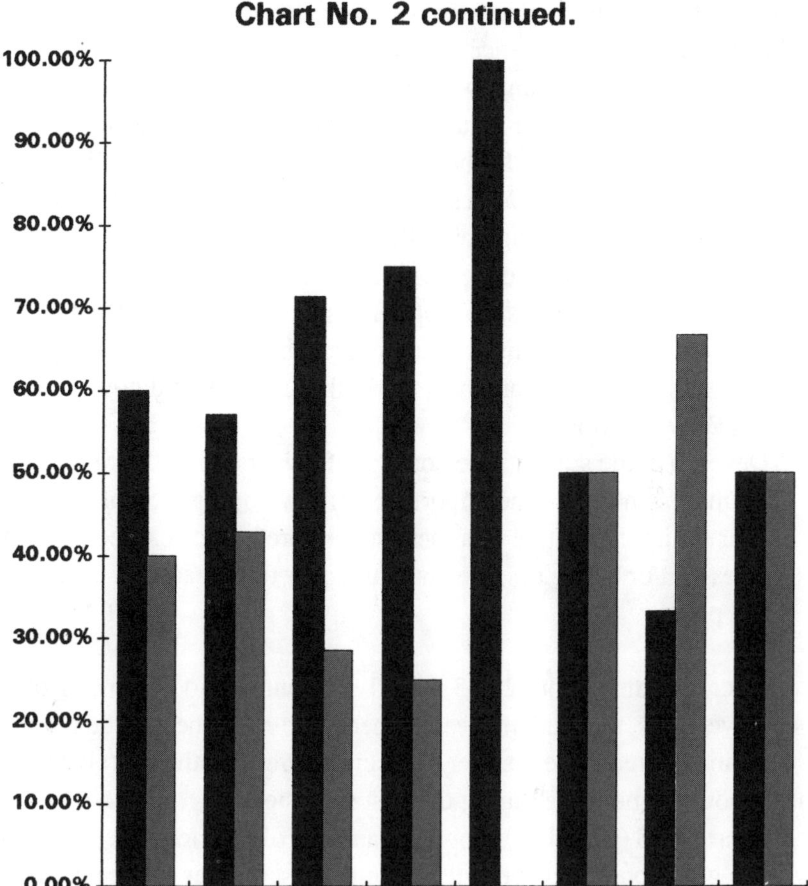

schools, the fear of corporal punishment no longer exists. Knowing that little can be done to them as students except kick them out of a place where they don't want to be, students really have few things to restrict their behavior. With all of the conflicts between the different temperaments within the schools, many students suffer from anger, apathy, low achievement, and low self-esteem.

Lacking an awareness as to how the human brain works and the true value of an education, students cannot be expected to make quality decisions about whether to participate fully in their classes.

9   Schools: The Problem

Working with 7th and 8th grade students it was decided to attempt to change the building-wide behavior and achievement levels of eighty-eight 7th grade science students. These students would be the test group and the other eighty seven 7th grade students who did not have science this semester would be the control group. The students in the test group were tested for hemisphere usage preference and instructed in the areas of brain structure, function, and downshifting, to try to achieve the following goals:

1.   Students will have an understanding of their own and other peoples' varying hemisphere usage preferences, and how these differing preferences affect feelings, thinking, and basic human interactions.
2.   Students will understand how the brain functions and how to control Downshifting.
3.   Develop in the students the concept of ownership of their brain and an understanding of the importance of developing their mind for their future, no matter what hemisphere preference caused philosophies and/or behaviors, are maintained by their teachers, parents, and peers.

After spending about 2 to 3 fifty-five minute periods working on the above goals, the students were expected to raise their grade point levels, and decrease the number of discipline reports they received throughout the building during the first semester.

Chart No. 3 (page 107) shows the amount of difference between the average grade point of each student for the last quarter of the previous school year, compared to the grade point average for first quarter of their present school year. The results were encouraging in both increased achievement, and with large numbers of students whose behavior improved building wide. This research was repeated the following three years and the students in the test group always had improved grades and behavior. Consider the possibilities. We could increase student and teacher self-esteem, and achievement levels. We could decrease discipline problems and drop-out rates, all by giving educators, students, and parents enough information on how the brain functions, so they can take ownership, control, and responsibility for their role in the educational system. The answer is to empower both the student and the teacher to a new freedom of choice through increased

Results of Research

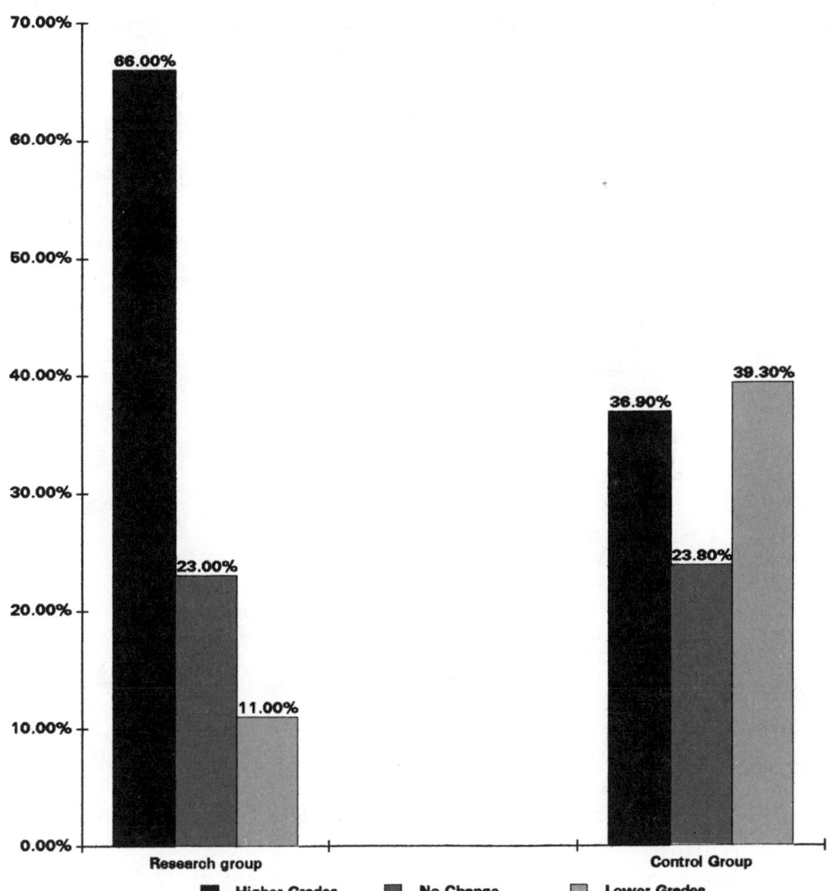

information and awareness.

Today's educational system must acknowledge and nurture the brain hemisphere usage preference differences of teachers and students. If it doesn't happen, the school system, and our society as a whole will pay for the apathy and anger currently seen in our schools. Do we stay the way we are? Or can we as individuals and as a society, through the knowledge gained from brain research and information on brain hemisphere usage preferences, put aside some of our own strong beliefs in order to increase the achievement and self esteem of others?

9 Schools: The Problem

As in the old proverb; a scorpion wanted to cross the river and stings the frog on whom he rides. As they are both drowning, the frog asks, "Why did you do this, now we will drown in the river!" The scorpion answers, "I can't help it, it's my nature."

If you reverse the statement, "You have to see it to believe it" to "You have to believe it to see it" you will be closer to seeing the problem. How do we get past "it's just my nature" to believing, seeing and working on the problem and its solution.

Chapter 10
SCHOOLS: THE SOLUTION

We have a problem, one that decreases self-esteem, decreases productivity, breaks up families, and derails the educational process for over 28% of our students nation-wide.

We should be able to accept a certain level of saying, no fault, no blame, for past behavior, but we can't afford to allow this to continue into the future.

So what do we do?

Isn't our problem the result of people lacking knowledge?

When the information in this book is presented in a 10 hour college class, people are astonished of the simplicity of the problem and at their own lack of knowledge after they have had so much training and previous educational experience.

So the answer seems to be that we need to spread this information throughout our society. When students are given this information it empowers them to increase their level of success and decrease their level of anger and anxiety. The same results are achieved when this material is shared with adults.

It is hoped this book will stimulate enough people in authoritative positions to take the bull by the horns and implement the program outlined here.

Here is a suggested method for decreasing many of our problems in a short time and most of them over a longer time.

1. Develop coordinated, goal oriented, and mass media presentations on:

    A. Brain structure and function

    B   What happens in the brain as we learn

    C. What causes our special aptitudes and talents

    D. Causes and effects of downshifting

    E. Causes of and needs for the diversity of different temperaments or types of people and their belief systems.

    F. "No Fault, No Blame" concept for past behavior with expression of self choice to be happy for the future.

2. Presentations and testing in churches, fraternal organizations, businesses, homes, schools, colleges, etc.

3. Strong media support by famous athletes, entertainers, politicians, etc.

4. Changes in the curriculum, testing methods, teaching methods, and discipline systems to create a more brain compatible and less discriminatory system.

5. Develop a media, school, and parent supported program to increase the value of an education in the eyes of our students.

6. Develop a media, school, and parent supported program to decrease discrimination and increase tolerance for family and community members who have inherited different abilities, needs and expectations.

If we can achieve this we will have a start. There will be those who disagree, but the choices are few. We cannot continue to travel down the same road; it is not morally or financially reasonable.

Chapter 11
THE BUSINESS WORLD

The Brain, Temperament Groups, and Downshifting vs Productivity

Each individual is born into this world with a specific preference to use specific areas of the brain to perceive and evaluate happenings in that persons' world. As with families and schools, the differing natural inherited brain area usage preferences of individuals within a business can cause many problems. Most members of the management team will be part of what is commonly called the SJ group or temperament. The needs and expectations of most of the members of the management team will be for employees to work at and finish tasks in a orderly, efficient, and business like manner. Normally, this will also include the expectation that all employees will follow and obey all procedures, rules, and regulations precisely. These expectations will also apply to all other members of the management team and to each individual's family members.

When employees fail to meet the management's needs and expectations the anxiety level of management will rise. If a member of the management team fails to meet the required expectations, conflict will also arise. This increased anxiety or anger can be expressed in many ways. The management's method of expressing its concern to create the needed change affects the productivity of the employees, the management team itself, and in the end, the entire business.

These attitudes can be compared directly to a person's student years. A search for a cause for the lack of achievement of students in a school found that 81.8% of students who were happy at home and school could achieve grades of a three point or better. If students were unhappy at home but happy at school, only 76% of the students could still achieve a three point grade or better. When students are unhappy at school, even if they are happy at home, only 50% of the students in this group can achieve a three point grade or above. If the students are unhappy at school and at home, only 20% of these student achieve a three point grade or better.

It seems very logical to most of us, when we take the time to think about it, that unhappy or angry children or adults will be less interested in doing high quality work. We all know that our work rate decreases when we are angry.

When we consider the fact that members of different temperaments downshift or get angry for different reasons and that each temperament has different needs and expectations, we can see that there is much opportunity for misunderstandings and disagreements leading to anxiety and anger. The chart on page 80 shows some of the major differences between the four major groups of temperaments.

As the chart shows, the needs and expectations of the different groups are diverse and many times the very opposite. It is natural for the people of different temperament to get irritated with each other. The problem is, since most people lack the knowledge of how their brain works, they have little control over their negative emotions and behaviors.

Consider the following statement:

"No freedom of choice without information."

Neither members of management nor employees can have true freedom of choice without knowledge of their brain and temperament.

You can not have complete control over productivity without the proper information. Presenting this information decreases anxiety and increases productivity in any organization.

The irritation and anger that affects the productivity of a business is not limited to relationships between management and employees. The individual relationships between all employees of a business affect the productivity of that business. Even the relationships in the families at home can cause individuals to be less productive on the job.

Even though the results of anxiety and anger are costly to a business, remember there is "no fault or blame" involved in this problem. It is mainly caused by a lack of information, which, in itself, is not a cure-all; it is a tool to help increase productivity.

Chapter 12
THE SELF HELP SECTION

This section of the book contains information that can be used for:

1. Helping individuals come to terms with and control their own behavior.
2. Helping individuals "upshift" themselves and others.
3. Helping individuals grasp the whole concept.

Having read the information contained in the first 11 chapters, in order to increase clarity, the following choices are available:

1. The Ethics Letter

The following is a letter that is handed out at all of my seminars. Its purpose is to warn people that indiscriminate use of this information can cause downshifting in those people close to you. It is best that you allow them to discover the material on their own.

FROM: Claude Beamish - Brain Research and Temperament Presenter

TO: Presentation Participants

A few ethical reminders. Please do not use temperament testing as a rock hard depiction of another person. The test I distributed and the one in the Keirsey and Bates book can be influenced by anger and emotion and by indecision when a person uses both hemispheres fairly equally. We all have a set of beliefs and methods for dealing with everyday life, caused by our brain hemisphere usage preferences. Try not to get locked into only your view point.

When astronauts of opposing countries combined in an orbiting space flight, the Russian astronaut said, "At the beginning we all individually pointed out our own continents and countries, but by the end of the flight we only saw one earth." In the beginning you might see individuals as having strong biases. In the end we hope you see individuals with different brain usage patterns, who honestly believe that what they say and do is best for the people they work with. If we can end up working together as a group of humans with a common goal and at the same time maximize the use of our special abilities, we will have a better life on this earth.

Try not to take what other people say and do personally. Think about how you would react and feel if you had an SJ, SP, NF, or NT set of beliefs.

Do not try guessing and labelling other teachers, family members, students, business associates, or friends.

Remember temperament testing is only a stepping stone to the acceptance of others and the cognitive ability of individuals to control downshifting. The controlling of downshifting should allow individuals to increase achievement and improve relationships with others.

The validation of all temperaments should raise the level of self-esteem and acceptance of all.

The chart on temperament groups and downshifting you received at the presentation (page 80) will give you some ideas on how to respond to people of different temperaments.

Here is a list of books, if you wish more information:

Hart, Leslie A., *Human Brain and Human Learning.*

Wonder and Donovan, *Whole-Brain Thinking: Working from Both Sides of the Brain.*

Keirsey and Bates, *Please Understand Me.*

2. No Fault, No Blame

Believe it or not, all of us in our own minds, in our own ways, are trying to get other people to do what we think will be good for them. We punish and hurt because we feel the other person needs to do things our way in order to succeed. We want so badly to help that we get angry and maybe even downshift to violence when we finally start concentrating on getting our way instead of trying to help. It is surprising how fast we take it extremely personally when people refuse to see our view point, which, as we know, is the right way to do something.

So here we are stuck in a world where most people out of the goodness of their hearts are trying to help us do things according to their "right way." Most of us naturally resent their interference, so we live our lives with stress and anger.

If you are viewing this No Fault, No Blame concept for the first time, try to forget and forgive yours and others misdeeds. If you can, try to go back and apologize to those people you have hurt. If other people in your life do not yet know about temperaments, modelling, and the problems they cause, try to be tolerant of their hurting attempts to help you. Never attempt to explain the problem to a person with whom you are in conflict. It would be better and more productive if they discovered the problem on their own by reading the book or using the computer program (see advertisement in back of the book). After the individuals involved have viewed the material, try to sit down and discuss each other's individual specific needs, beliefs, and expectations.

3. The Big Picture:

Temperaments, Needs, Expectations, Anger, and Choices

Each person on this earth has his or her own unique temperament or personality. Their temperament is a result of a specific brain usage pattern which was inherited from their parents and strengthened or weakened by their environment during the growing up years.

Because of inherited temperament, each brain of each human has special needs, expectations, and abilities. They are the result of a specific pattern of usage within that individual's brain as it handles the processes of Thought Grounding, Perceiving, Evaluation, and Primary Brain Orientation. These needs, expectations, and abilities differ from person to person.

When the needs and expectations of an individual are not met or when a person does not have a needed ability, the individual's brain can do a process called downshifting. Downshifting involves a movement within the individual's brain, down to a lower, older, and faster-acting portion of the brain to handle this crisis of unmet needs and expectations or missing abilities. This lower and older portion of the brain does not have the abilities, insights, or controls of our upper Neo-Cortex or advanced human brain.

When an individual is in this downshifted mode we would say that they are in some stage of anger or frustration. In this mode, we do not have the same abilities, insights, or controls. Therefore, many times we tend to make bad decisions: such as saying things we wouldn't normally say or basically getting ourselves into trouble with other people. The normal cycle between humans is that when one person downshifts into anger because of unmet needs and expectations, the resulting behavior or actions will downshift the other person involved.

The result is two people fighting with each other, both working at the intellectual and control level of a rhinoceros. With neither person having control over what is said or done, the outlook is negative and may often lead to violence, as the brain downshifts even further down to a still older and less controlled area in order to try to win or hurt. Another possible result is, if this conflict happens too often, the people will cease to want to be around each other. The sensitivity can become so great that the two people can even start to downshift at the sight of each other.

Violence, divorces, yelling, and screaming are all because of unmet needs and expectations. But a person's needs and expectations are basically a part of that person's own inherited temperament. So how can it be wrong? How can any one person's inherited needs and expectations be more important or more right or wrong than another person's inherited needs or expectations? Both people are trapped in a brain which has a tendency to see the world in its own specific way and also feels bad when its needs and expectations are not met.

But are we actually talking about rights and wrongs? Each person has his or her set of standards, beliefs, and philosophies depending on the inherited brain area usage preferences combined with all the knowledge stored in the brain. The problem is not who is right or wrong. There are no right or wrongs to most issues, just different ways of viewing situations or problems. But nonetheless we judge other people we believe are wrong. They need to be corrected, because our temperament controlled brain says that what, how, or that they are or are not doing something, is incorrect.

There are many ways of doing things, who is to say what is the perfect or right way?

Male to male and female to female, we search throughout our world to find a person that has a similar brain usage pattern to be our friend. This person as our friend with a like temperament very seldom disagrees with us. More important, this person continually validates and supports the idea that what we think is really right. The more we feel we are right the stronger our negative judging is and the quicker we downshift to anger. This can be a devastating cycle especially since 75% of the time, when we marry, we tend to marry a person who has our opposite temperament. This person will have a hard time meeting our opposite needs and expectations. Out of the mistaken belief that what we think is the only right, we could live in almost continual anger and upset and end up driving people, even family members, away from us.

In marriages, you have two people committed to a partnership. The problem is that most people do not realize that they now have two sets of possibly opposite needs and expectations to try and satisfy.

Two basic human drives are: pleasing ourselves and ownership. As we progress through life each individual reaches different levels of the ability to please others and the ability to give to others. Depending upon each individual's temperament and level of mental and emotional development those involved can either continue to live and support each other in happiness, or through competition, downshift into anger over their natural differences.

Each person in a marriage will also bring learned expectations from the person's early family life.

If possible, in order to avoid confrontation, couples should talk over their ideas on raising a family before they get married. If either person or both get locked into a negative cycle of judging and worrying about who does how much, the marriage will be in for problems. Each partner needs to have the strength to allow the other person some freedom to be herself or himself while at the same time appreciating each other's individual needs and expectations.

In schools, the single-mindedness of students, teachers, and administrators with differing temperaments causes downshifting and anger. There is an even greater problem in the school setting: when a student is downshifted to the rhino brain, the student loses the ability to take in information and learn. This downshifting can be caused by disagreeing with another person or actually having an inherited deficit which continually frustrates the student, while being downgraded by others. Everyone knows of students who got As in the classes where they liked the teacher or were good at the subject, and Fs or Ds in the classes where they disliked the teacher or had disabilities that lowered their success in that subject. This varying of achievement, that correlates with downshifting or lack of downshifting, shows how greatly our school success is negatively affected by mismatches of temperaments, judging, disabilities and the I'm right syndrome.

It is important to know how our brains function during stress or anxiety. When we do, we can see that there is a fine line or a controllable moment in time between downshifted irrational anger and being the person we should, could, or would be by staying in our upper more advanced human brain. We have a choice. We have the power to choose to stay in our upper brain. We can choose to be more tolerant. We can choose to be less judging of others. Through these choices we can gain more happiness for ourselves and those around us.

In order for each of us to reach our fullest potential and remain in a happy state of mind, we must accept who we are and gain control over the functioning of our brain. The key to reaching our full potential and remaining happy is to value our abilities and realize that most other people do not think as we do. For the largest groups of people who have like brain usage patterns there is still 79% of the population that would probably disagree with them.

People in other temperaments do not deal with the world in the same way we do and are usually unaware of how their behavior is affecting or hurting people of our temperament. Most people usually just live their lives making decisions their particular brain organization decides is right.

Don't take decisions or actions different from yours as a sign of lack of caring or lack of love. People can be in love and still see the world differently. Remember, almost 75% of the time we chose to marry a person who has opposite ways of handling life's problems.

Don't take a lesser ability in any activity as an immovable barrier to future happiness. All individuals have their own specific abilities. We all need to stay in the upper brain and work hard to do our best. If we want to and work hard, we can learn almost anything.

It doesn't seem fair but we are trapped in our brain and can very easily, because of our ego, get into competition with those around us. For some reason having to be right can get so important that we may lose our friends, children, spouses, and jobs just so we can feel we won.

In reality it seems to come down to having to be right and fighting genetic differences with downshifting or accepting that we are different on purpose, accepting others' rights to think and act differently and staying happy.

In a situation where you are starting to downshift or get angry, ask yourself the following questions:

1. Are the actions or behaviors of the person involved something being done to you or just an inherited natural behavior?
2. If it is an inherited natural behavior, is it something the other person needs to be aware of and change or do you need to accept the person for who that person is?
3. Does the person involved know that what has been said or done has bothered you?
4. Does what they have said or done mean what you think it means? If you don't know, politely and in a friendly manner ask the person what was meant.
5. Is what has happened important enough to worry about?

6. If the person meant what was said or done, is the person important enough in your life to be worth getting angry, upset, or hurt over?
7. If the person is that important, can you discuss the problem in a caring non-downshifted manner?

This might seem hard to do, but when you look at all the negative alternatives, it is worth a try. Being unhappy, angry, and downshifted over genetically caused differences only leads to further problems for us to handle. If you are downshifted and angry because you cannot get other people to see it your way, you probably feel like you are beating your head against a brick wall and you probably are. For most of us life is what we make it, whether we realize it or not. The choice is ours. We can end up fighting another person's heredity-directed needs, expectations, and behaviors through downshifting; or we can accept that we are different on purpose, accept others' rights to think and act differently, support one another, and be happy.

4. Victims

Being a victim is an interesting concept. Each of us is a victim during the times when we confront individuals with beliefs, behaviors, or philosophies different from ours. One or both of us gets angry. Stress, anxiety, anger, and hurt accumulate in our lives. These negative feelings decrease our productivity and self-esteem and by creating large areas of stress and strain, lead directly to shortening our lives.

Because our individual brain usage patterns are different from those of other people, we, all of us, as individuals can spend a large portion of our lives angry with other people in our lives. Without the knowledge that people are naturally genetically different, we can spend a large amount of time feeling sorry for ourselves, while at the same time trying to make other people think, act, and feel as we do.

When we marry, get a job, have children, make friends, or in any other way have to spend time with others, our own specific needs, beliefs, and expectations get in the way. We normally judge and evaluate other people's actions, ideas, knowledge levels, beliefs, and behaviors by comparing them to our own. If they do not come up to our standards or wishes, we are unhappy. Little do we know it, but the other person is doing the same thing to us. And guess what, we don't measure up either. The usual result of this is one or both people down-shifting into anger, rebellion, or even into violence.

If you can see how different temperaments react to the world so differently, you will understand that we are all victims. As each of us lives in this world, we are each hurt to some extent. When husbands and wives fight, everyone in the family is a victim. Then through modeling and more inherited temperaments the victimizing is passed on to the next generation.

There is an American Indian proverb that says: "Do not judge any man until you have walked two moons in his moccasins." Try to see how other people view the situation. Try to walk in the other person's moccasins, realizing that others too are trapped in their temperaments as you are in yours. It may not be fair, but until we can overcome our anger and tendency to judge others, we will all continue to be victims.

5. Percentages of temperament letters

LEFT HEMISPHERE			RIGHT HEMISPHERE	
F				
E	75%	E	25%	I
M	75%	S	25%	N
A	25%	T	75%	F
L	50%	J	50%	P
E				
M	75%	E	25%	I
A	75%	S	25%	N
L	75%	T	25%	F
E	50%	J	50%	P

6. Percentages of temperaments

In the charts below you will find your temperament letters. Above each column of temperament letters is a number representing the percentage of people of your sex and temperament in our society. If you multiply the top number above each column by the number of temperaments listed below it, then add up the results of all four columns you should get one hundred percent. Because the female brain is different than the male brain, there are two distinct charts. Be sure you are looking at the right chart.

Female

21%	7%	2.4%	.8%
	ENFJ	INFJ	
	ENFP	INFP	
ESFJ	ESTJ	ENTJ	INTJ
ESFP	ESTP	ENTP	INTP
	ISFJ	ISTJ	
	ISFP	ISTP	

Male

21%	7%	2.4%	.8%
	ENTJ	ENFJ	
	ENTP	ENFP	
ESTJ	ISTJ	INTJ	INFJ
ESTP	ISTP	INTP	INFP
	ESFJ	ISFJ	
	ESFP	ISFP	

7. Choosing friends and marriage partners

Because of your particular inherited brain usage pattern, you have your specific needs, beliefs, and expectations.

When choosing best friends of the same sex we usually try find a person who has the same temperament or brain usage pattern as ours. We need support for our temperament and we need to have other people agree with our needs, beliefs, and expectations.

As young children starting out in school we search throughout the school for someone who has our same brain organization. By continually sifting through all the students at school, year after year, we will possibly find a best friend who will continually validate and support our way of life.

In Percentages of temperaments above, you can see that two of the temperaments for each sex only exist in .8% of the population. Two other temperaments for each sex have the largest numbers of similar temperaments and make up 21% of the population. This means that even for people with the most common temperaments 79% of the population will not support or validate many of their needs, beliefs, and expectations. People in the .8% group tend to feel very lonely and misunderstood. They will have a hard time finding best friends sharing their own uncommon temperament, who can validate their lives. This is because 99.2% of the general population will not understand or validate the life styles of the .8%. People of uncommon temperaments, because of lack of support in early life, will commonly have a low self-esteem, making it even harder to approach other people in order to make close friends.

In choosing a husband or a wife, the situation is very different. 75% of the time, we choose a person with an almost opposite brain hemisphere usage pattern or opposite temperament. This seems to be purely a genetically controlled subconscious decision. It happens in order to fill a need for our species continually to mix the gene pool, rather than making specific groups by continually marrying someone of our own temperament.

As a result of choosing a mate who has our opposite temperament, we must live with a person who does not have our same needs, beliefs, and expectations. Therefore most of us have a partner who most often cannot or does not validate our beliefs, satisfy our needs, or meet our expectations. Being married to our opposite temperament can lead to much anxiety and anger. Even if we end up divorcing our first opposite, we will more than likely go right back out and choose another partner who is our opposite temperament to start the negative process all over again.

8. Modeling and Your Early Environment

If we look at our present way of living or behaving and compare it to how our parents lived, we probably will find one of two things. First, as an individual, if we did not consciously disagree with our parents' way of living or behaving, we are probably living or behaving much like the parent of our own sex and if married expecting our spouse to act like our other parent.

Second, if, because of our temperament, we consciously disagreed with our parents' behavior or way of life, we are probably living and behaving as oppositely as we can. Either one of these tendencies could be self-destructive.

124

Let's look at some examples.

If a boy grows up with a workaholic father and learns that hard work and no play is the proper way to live, he can live his father's life never realizing that life should have some fun parts. He would also use this modeled way of life to dictate and judge the behaviors of all the other people in his life as a grown man. This person may even feel guilty if he has fun and be upset with others who want to have fun.

The next son living with this father may end up the same way or if his temperament says that this is not fair, the son may go overboard the opposite way, making sure he has fun in his life and avoid getting serious about work.

If a boy or girl grows up in a family where the parent of their sex is either absent or irresponsible, the child could have the same tendencies as an adult. If such children view their parents' behavior as unfair they may go overboard trying to be always present and super responsible, thus restricting their own lives.

When a child is subject to severe emotional, physical, verbal, or sexual abuse, as an adult that child will subconsciously have a low self-esteem because of what they have been through and because they incorrectly feel it was the fault of the child within. This subconscious low self-esteem may show itself through some common characteristic abnormal behaviors. Adults who had abusive parents may over-eat, over-drink, or take drugs to make themselves less appealing to others or to block the pain they feel. They also may marry far beneath their own abilities, or an abusive person to prove further their low self-worth, or to punish themselves. This self destructive behavior is accomplished by the subconscious mind without any conscious awareness of the real reasons. The adult probably does not even consciously remember that the abuse took place, or know that, subconsciously, he or she incorrectly feels responsibility for that abuse. Because of such persons' low self-esteem they can be very abusive to their own family members while simultaneously needing or demanding continual respect and caring. A young child living with this child abuse victim may suffer the same way, thus perpetuating the problem.

Think about your life and compare it to your parents' behaviors. Make sure you are not hurting yourself or others because you are unnecessarily living a life that is the result of modeling or anti-modeling your parents.

9. The Black Sheep Syndrome

Parents want it. Teachers want it. Students want it. Politicians want it. When we think about it, we would all like to see ourselves and other people productive and happy. We would like to reduce crime, decrease the use of drugs, reduce the dropout levels in our schools, and generally decrease the amount of money spent on fighting these societal problems.

The problem is that most of us seem to have an incorrect assumption. We tend to think that, if other people could just do things better or if they could only see and do things our way, everything would work out fine. Because of these feelings and beliefs, we push harder and harder to get people to see the light—*our light!*

One group of people make a rule or pass a law and another group of people, because they disagree, rebel against it or fight to change the rule or law. Disagreements between people or groups of people over personal points of view results in decreased learning, decreased productivity, increased violence, and sometimes even deaths.

Finally we need to see that most of these differences in viewpoint come from genetically caused differences in the usage patterns within the brains of all of us. This lack of knowledge creates major problems. By using different areas of our brains to perceive and process information, we come up with many different sets of behaviors, needs, aptitudes, beliefs, expectations, and philosophies.

Each child arrives in this world with preset tendencies to use specific areas in the brain in order to react to the environment. Thus the child perceives and evaluates the surroundings in that child's own specific way. The child will also have specific needs and expectations.

Many children get along fine in their environment. When their needs and expectations are met they grow and mature into successful adults. Other children, because of their unmet special needs and expectations, seem to be almost allergic to their environment. This allergic tendency leaves these children in a situation where lack of success and increased anger are most common. Because of a child's or an adult's rebelliousness and not fitting in, the individual may be referred to as the black sheep of the family. The sad part of this is that if the individual had been born into a family whose members had needs and expectations closer to his or hers, the child would have been considered as normal, not the black sheep.

The action of anger has some very important negative side effects. Unknown to most people is the fact that with anger comes an inability to learn, to listen, to evaluate logically, and an inability to control emotions. This is caused by the physical act of moving to a lower part of the brain (downshifting) to handle a negatively perceived situation. And because children arrive in this world with many preset needs and expectations that are hard for some parents to meet, these children are set up for anger, lack of success, and low self-esteem. The lack of self-esteem comes from the lack of success and the lack of validation. The lack of success is one of the results of anger. Since angry students use a lower older portion of the brain, they lose the ability to learn.

The lack of control over emotions, combined with the inability to evaluate clearly the situations, leads to negative self-destructive actions that further inflame the situations. This happens over and over again leading to a negative spiral of anger and decreased success and decreased happiness for the student and the many other people involved in the student's life.

The biggest problem our society has is that most people lack knowledge about the brain, and that leaves many people in one of these negative spirals. All of the anger-based negative spirals contribute to the increase of unemployment, illiteracy, crime, poverty, and drug abuse. The cost of fighting these problems is almost crippling our society.

It has been proven that just the cognitive awareness of our natural differences combined with the knowledge of the negative effects of anger can allow students to avoid negative spirals and achieve success and greater self-esteem. Once people know the reason for their anger and its negative effects, they simply refuse to be bothered by other people's differences, thus choosing to learn and be successful.

10. Further Development of Your Brain

You have a natural tendency to be able to learn certain subjects or perform certain tasks better than other people. This is a result of an inherited tendency for your brain to myelinate or coat nerve cells in specific areas of your brain with fat. This fat is for insulation purposes to allow cells to communicate more clearly and at a faster rate. Depending on which areas of your brain are myelinated, you have your special talents or abilities. You do not have any control over which areas are myelinated. It is determined by genetics, those characteristics handed down to you from your parents. What you can do is develop what you have by developing or strengthening both your strong and weak areas.

The human brain is developed or strengthened through the process of adding dendrites. The more dendrites you have per nerve cell in each portion of your brain the more knowledge or ability you have in that subject or activity.

Through continual downshifting or the act of not being interested in learning, many people do not participate in the *system for developing dendrites*, commonly called school.

Don't worry. It's not too late. The brain can add new dendrites at anytime, at any age, as long as you are alive. People have gone to college at the age of ninety and earned new doctorate degrees.

If you have a hard time reading, either go to a literacy class or just start reading any material. If you keep it up you will connect more and more dendrites in your brain and it will become easier and easier to read. This will work with any subject, the more you work at any subject, the easier it will become.

If you are a person who is right hemisphere dominant, with a majority of your temperament letters being I, N, F, and P, you will need to work at the tasks of organization, finishing, and being on time.

If you are a person who is left hemisphere dominant, having a majority of your temperament letters being E, S, T, and J, you will need to work at gaining more ability in the areas of flexibility, creativity, spontaneity, caring, adapting, and imagination.

As far as developing talents you might lack in areas like spelling, art, memorizing, etc., books like *Making the Most of Your Mind*, by Tony Buzan or any of the other available books on developing both hemispheres of the brain are recommended reading.

Remember the ability of your brain to learn and develop is almost unlimited. Stay upshifted. Pay attention and learn. It's your brain and it is your responsibility to develop your brain.

Nobody can make you learn and nobody else is responsible if you do not develop your brain. To be angry and downshifted over differences in natural inherited needs and expectation only stops you from learning and being happy. It seems like an awful destructive thing to do to yourself.

What you do, whether you learn, what you earn, where you go, and whether you are happy in this world is up to you!

11. Occupations

The specific occupations where you find higher percentages of people of your personality will be found on the following charts.

If the first letter of your four temperament letters is an I for Introvert, look for occupations on the Introvert chart.

If the first letter of your four temperament letters is an E for Extrovert, look for occupations on the Extrovert chart.

The number that proceeds each occupation tells you the number of times more often your type of person is found in that occupation. For example both the INFP and the INFJ have the number 4 in front of fine arts. This means that INFJs and INFPs have four times as many people as in the normal population in the area of fine arts. This is one of the reasons why there is a statement in their profile that says: It is highly probable that you have artistic talents.

Occupations vs Temperaments for Introverts

ISTJ	ISFJ	INFJ	INTJ
4 Police	3 Designers	4.5 Clergy	5 Architects
4 Bank employee	3 Sister	4 Fine artists	4 Attorneys admin.
3 Steel workers	3 Clerical super.	3 Psychodram.	4 Consultants
3 Managers	2 Administrator	3 Social workers	4 Lawyers
3 Principals	2 Book keepers	2 Psychologists	4 Chemists
3 Accountants	2 Police	2 English teacher	3 Judges
3 School bus dri.	2 Doctors general	2 Architects	3 Photographers
3 Federal exec.	2 Probation off.	2 Preschool teach.	3 Federal exec.
3 Corrections sgt.	2 Bank employees	2 Librarians	3 Chemical eng.
3 Purchasing agt.	2 Teacher elem.	2 Counselor	3 Research worker
2 Administrators	2 Guards		3 Accountants
2 Electricians	2 Doctor osteop.		3 Psychologists
2 Math teacher	2 Teacher preschool		3 Dentists
2 Chemists	2 Cashiers		3 Electrical eng.
2 Dentists	2 Nursing		2 Acting, musician
2 Auditors	2 Librarians		2 Auditors
2 Mechanical eng.	2 Teachers aids		2 Principals
2 Electronic eng.	2 School bus driver		2 Reporter, editor
2 Consultants	2 Cashiers		2 Biologists
2 Coal miners	2 Typists		2 Writers
2 Computer anyl.	2 Hair dressers		2 Entertainer
	2 Corrections sgt.		2 Administrator
	2 Child care		2 Journalist

ISTP	ISFP	INFP	INTP
4 Police	3 Surveyor	4 Fine artists	4 Consultants
3 Steel workers	3 Sale people	3 Counselors	4 Chemists
3 Farmers	3 Clerical super.	3 Psychologists	3 Architect
3 Surveyors	2 Carpenters	3 Architect	3 Lawyer
3 Construction	2 Cooks	2 Journalist	3 Research assist.
3 Carpenters	2 Police	2 Carpenters	3 Surveyors
2 Cooks	2 Typists	2 Reporter, editor	3 Fine artists
2 Typists	2 Dental assist.	2 Lab. tech.	2 Judges
2 Dental assist.	2 Construction	2 Writers	2 Biologist
2 Craftworkers	2 Electrician	2 Physical therap.	2 Psychologist
2 Coal miner		2 English teacher	2 Acting
		2 Acting	2 Research anal.
		2 Cooks	2 Designers
			2 Psychiatrists
			2 Sales agent

Occupations vs Temperaments for Extroverts

ESTP	ESFJ	ENFP	ENTP
4 Marketing	3 Sales people	3 Social work	4 Photographer
3 Police	3 Child care	3 Psychodram.	3 Marketing
3 Carpenters	2 Cashiers	3 Counselors	3 Sales Agent
3 Sales people	2 Designers	2 Clergy	3 Journalists
3 Craftworkers	2 Receptionists	2 Journalists	3 Acting
2 Guards	2 Clerical super.	2 Psychologists	3 Lawyers
2 Farmers	2 Electricians	2 Writers	3 Psychiatry
2 Construction		2 Receptionist	2 Sales
		2 Research assist.	2 Entertainers
		2 Fine artists	2 Biologists
		2 Surveyors	2 Research anyl.
		2 Dental hygenist	2 Writers
			2 Engineers
			2 Judges
			2 Farmers
			2 Electricians
			2 Construction
			2 Child care

ESTJ	ESFP	ENFJ	ENTJ
4 Managers	2 Bank employees	4 Clergy	5 Consultants
3 Police	2 Book keepers	3 Teacher	4 Research anyl.
3 Bank employees	2 Receptionists	3 Acting	4 Admin. attorney
3 School bus driv.	2 Typists	2 Designers	3 Marketing
3 Principals	2 Secretaries	2 Counselor	3 Administrators
3 Purchasing agt.	2 Nuns	2 Fine artists	3 Lawyers
3 Administrators	2 Child care	2 Entertainers	3 Biologists
2 Auditors	2 Hair dressers	2 Musician	2 Research assist.
2 Accountants	2 Clergy	2 Composers	2 Acting
2 Consultants	2 Dental assist.	2 Consultants	2 Designer
2 Mech. engineer		2 Psychodramatist	2 Principals
2 Steel worker		2 Pharmacist	2 Psychologist
2 Farmers		2 Optometrist	2 Judges
2 Coal miners		2 Writers	2 Dentists
2 Judges			2 Probation offic.
2 Chem. engineers			2 English teacher
2 Corrections sgt.			2 Managers
2 Federal exec.			2 Accountants
2 Cooks			2 Chemists

12. To the student

Before you read this section, be sure you have read both *Victims* and *No Fault, No Blame*, (pages 121, 116).

The following chart was used during the research in the 7th and 8th grade science classes:

> This is your life, you have grown
> from a united egg and sperm into the
> person you are now. You have your
> own individual abilities. No matter
> what your home life is like, whether
> you have many or few friends, what
> you do with your life is up to you.
> Putting all other things aside, you have
> to decide to work and develop your
> own abilities. Work now, while you
> are in school, and you will have it eas-
> ier for the rest of your life.

Remember the brain can only learn and connect dendrites when you are not downshifted. If you are downshifting or getting angry because most of the people, out of the goodness of their heart, are trying to help you do things according to their right way, try to remember, when you downshift, you can't learn.

Students of specific freedom and fairness orientations are set up for failure in our school systems. Do not allow anger to rob you of your education. Remember *No Fault, No Blame*. Each teacher in his or her own way is trying to get you to follow what is seen as the "right" path to success. Each person of each temperament can learn anything he or she wants to learn. Work hard while you are in school. Don't fight to win against the system and end up losing the education and quality of life you deserve.

13. Normal student or child behaviors by groups

The following lists of characteristics are those that can be used to help students understand their special needs and problems. The descriptions can also be used in conjunction with the pitfall lists of the four major groups to empower students to make their choices of whether to downshift or stay in the upper brain and learn. A comparison discussion of the needs and normal (negative or positive) behaviors of each of the four groups of students can lead to more tolerance and acceptance within a large group of students.

Characteristics of the SJ child or student

SJs are sensitive to things being finished or going as planned, as explained or as rules dictate. They will probably complain when things don't.

They live in the moment; reactions to statements and/or behaviors may be immediate and intense.

They need predictable, stable, structured, and safe family and peer relationships.

They can become extremely distraught or depressed when they have unstable family, school, or peer relationships.

They may correct other peoples' statements or behaviors, even their teachers or parents who are not doing what they said they would be doing.

They are usually described as that "neat kid!" since they usually get what we want done and usually follow rules.

They may end up shouldering the burdens of other students or family members who do not have the responsibility skills of this temperament.

When these students have anxiety, their into-the-moment temperament makes them feel that there is no way out. Not being Intuitors, they have a hard time escaping to the future or to daydreaming. This causes intense stress and may cause a fight or flight reaction.

They usually have their work finished and well organized.

If you find an SJ who is having serious problems in school, you have probably found a student having some intense family, peer, or drug problems.

Some ISFJs, if they are a combination of a high Introvert and an extremely high Feeler, may be slow to mature. This is because they may not participate in school or with their peers because of their fear of being embarrassed or rejected.

SJs can be helpful students who like to clean, organize material, correct tests, lead activities (if extroverted) and teach other students.

Characteristics of the SP child or student

SPs are very sensitive to their need for freedom to do what they want to do when they want to do it.

They have a tendency to live in the present, not worrying about tomorrow, feeling that today must be enjoyed.

Positive or negative happenings or statements cause intense responses from SPs.

SPs may have problems finishing things or staying on task, unless it is something they want to do.

They can have extremely deep concentration on tasks they like. This can lead to very fine quality work or performances.

They can show rebelliousness at home, in school, in dress, in grooming, etc.

For many SPs the drive to separate from parental control is early and insistent. This can lead to considerable friction and anger in the home.

SPs are extremely fraternal and loyal to their friends

Many SPs may give freely to their friends, even their clothes, money, food, etc.

They can make decisions spontaneously, some of which will be self- destructive.

They are usually happy and helpful students when the teacher is liked and asks for help or cooperation instead of demanding it.

When angered the Extroverted SP may lose control and start yelling or leaving.

When angered the Introverted SP may clam up and be quiet, while seething with inner anger. In the classroom or at home this anger will be expressed in the form of continual defiance or by being a continual irritation to the person in charge. When and if the built up anger is released, it will be in one giant outburst, leaving those present wondering what happened to cause this reaction.

Too many strongly enforced rules is the quickest way to lose SP students' participation in any situation.

When participating in an activity they like such as band, art, athletics, shop, etc., these students can be extremely talented and happy if they like the teacher or coach.

Characteristics of the NF child or student

NFs continually question their own value or self-worth.

They are very sensitive to peoples' emotions towards them.

They are hurt very easily by indifference or anger.

They can have a questioning, inquisitive, what-when- and-why nature.

They have a holistic view needing to and being able to see the whole picture.

Their emotions are immediate and intense, whether expressed or not; they can be moody.

Their thought processing goes through Feelings in the associative right hemisphere. Likes and dislikes are important.

They look for possibilities.

The past is always present while they are looking to the future. They may have a hard time concentrating on the present.

They need continual support and praise.

They are easily downshifted by yelling.

They worry about other peoples' problems; they are caring children.

High ENFPs can become argumentative and show rebelliousness in clothing, grooming, etc.

Extremely downshifted INFPs or ENFPs will act like SPs, not wanting to be told what to do.

Extremely Downshifted INFJs and ENFJs will act like SJs, worry-ing about rules and correct procedures.

Some Introverted NFs may seem very immature. Their possible low self-esteem is caused by continual questioning of their self-value.

Introverted NFs do not like to have attention drawn to them. They tend to be very quiet in class and they may not answer questions because of their fear of embarrassment or rejection.

Characteristics of the NT child or student

NTs continually question their own and other's knowledge and abil-ities. This can cause a self-doubting attitude for themselves and towards others.

They are very sensitive to people's evaluation of their knowledge or talents. If they think they may not be correct, capable, or competent, NTs will probably avoid participating.

NTs have a questioning, inquisitive, what-when-and-how nature. They might irritate other people with their continual questions.

They have a holistic view and need to see and have the ability to see the whole picture.

Their evaluative thinking mode goes through the logical left hemisphere.

They have a need to know and a quick insight into how things work. They may continually take things apart.

Their emotions are hidden whether intense or not.

They can be argumentative and correcting of others. If they are continually rebuked they can get in a continual downshifted mode. During this time they may seem to have a chip on their shoulder.

They can feel different and be treated as different or not be accepted by others: the "brain," the "nerd," etc.

They may have problems with handwriting or language skills.

They can show rebelliousness in dress or grooming. All laws and rules must be justified in order to be accepted without downshifting.

They have an unusually strong preoccupation with fairness.

Some Introverted NTs may mature slowly. This is because of their continual questioning of their own abilities and their tendency not to fit into their peer group.

The combination of their need to be right and their use of their intuitive right hemisphere creates a tendency for NTs to be good at debating and they may tend to argue or debate with others.

14. Other temperaments and their characteristics

People of other temperaments have the same or a greater strength of conviction as you do, each person seeing the world, evaluating, and judging all from each individual's inherited or modeled perspective. Each is ready to fight and if pushed far enough, even ready to die for the way things are seen, even though it is just one of many ways of viewing the world.

Read and study the views of each of the four major groups. See how other people perceive the world.

If friends or relatives are willing, let them take the test. When they have read and agreed with their profiles and the characteristics of their major group, read their information and let them read yours. Increased understanding will bring more tolerance and happiness into your life.

15. Male vs Female: the Brain and the Body

This concept was not presented earlier because it would have clouded issues. In reality we need to work with who we are, not how we got there. On the other hand with certain knowledge we might be able to understand some issues in the present and avoid some problems in the future.

The difference between male and female has many facets. First there is the brain itself. The differences between the male and female brains cause all sorts of problems in the areas of communication and meeting needs between spouses or close friends who have an oppositely sexed brain. The female brain has an enlarged Corpus Callosum which is used to allow the two hemispheres better to communicate with each other. This is necessary because females use both hemispheres to work on most tasks. Males have a smaller Corpus Callosum. This is because the male brain basically uses only one or the other of the hemispheres to work on each individual task. These physical differences account for some general differences in behavior and ability between males and females.

In the section on page 122, you saw that 25% of males are Feelers and 25% of females are Thinkers. The members of these two groups of 25% can have many of the characteristics and abilities of their opposite sex.

75% of the males tend to be more serious, competitive, and able to concentrate deeply on one task. 75% of the females are more worried about harmony, relationships with others, and bring all areas of thought to a task.

Another difference between males and females is in their bodies. Males generally convert protein into muscle. Whereas females have a tendance to change it to fat to store for a possible reproductive cycle. The concept of male vs female bodies might seem quite apparent, but there is a reason it was brought up. The sex and type of body a human has is determined genetically by females receiving two X chromosomes and a male receiving an X and a Y chromosome. The brain is then caused to change to its appropriate male or female structure by the release or non-release from the genitals of the baby itself of reproductive chemicals such as testosterone and estrogen.

If anything interferes with the release of the appropriate chemicals, you could end up having a child born who has a male body with a female brain or a female body with a male brain. Two conditions have been linked to these situations. Pregnant females who are under severe stress can release hormones which block the production of testosterone in the fetus causing a male child to be born with a female type brain. This has also been found to occur with children of specific types of drug users. There are also situations which will cause females to be born with a male type of brain. The children born into these situations face all sorts of emotional, sexual, and social problems. Being in the minority they will face much undeserved discrimination. No children have personal control over the choice of their genetics or over what happens to them in the womb. How can society continue to allow such large amounts of discrimination against those who are uncontrollably different?

The last big difference between males and females, and even between males and males or females and females is the blood level of testosterone. Researchers have found that certain males are born with an increased level of testosterone production. This causes increased competitiveness and aggression leading to violence in many cases. There is a direct correlation between criminals and high levels of test-osterone. Testosterone is the fuel for aggression. Whether you are male or female the level of testosterone production will increase your levels of independence, individualism, self-assurance, and self-sufficiency.

16. You have choices

The following is an overhead used during my presentations, college classes, and seminars:

There is a Fine Line or a
Controllable Moment in Time
Between
Downshifted Irrational "Rhino" Anger
and being the person
you
SHOULD
COULD
or
WOULD
be.

You have CHOICES

We can choose to be happier. We can choose to be more tolerant. Being unhappy, angry, and downshifted over genetically caused differences only leads to further problems for us to handle. If you are downshifted and angry because you cannot get other people to see it your way, you probably feel like you are beating your head against a brick wall and you probably are. For most of us life is what we make it, whether we realize it or not. The choice is ours. We can end up fighting another person's heredity-directed needs, expectations, and behaviors through downshifting. The alternative is accepting that we are different on purpose, accepting others' rights to think and act differently, supporting one another, and being happy.

You need to make the choice!

BIBLIOGRAPHY

Armstrong T. (1987) *In Their Own Way*, Los Angeles: J. P. Tarcher, Inc.

Buzan T. (1977, 1984) *Make the Most of Your Mind*, New York: Simon & Schuster

Diamond M. (1988) *Enriching Heredity*, New York: Free Press

Gazzaniga M. S. (1988) *Mind Matters*, Boston: Houghton Mifflin

Hart L. A. (1983) *Human Brain and Human Learning*, New York: Brain Age Publishers

Hart L A. (1975) *How The Brain Works*, New York: Basic Books, Inc.

Keirsey D. and Bates M. (1978, 1984), *Please Understand Me* ,Del Mar, CA: Prometheus Nemesis Book Company

Lozanov G. (1978, 1989) *Suggestology and Outlines of Suggestopedy*, New York: Gordon and Breach Science Publishers

Meisgeier C. abd Murphy E. (1987) Manual: *Type Indicator for Children*, Palo Alto CA: Consulting Psychologists Press

Myers, I. (1962) Manual: *The Myers-Briggs Type Indicator*, Palo Alto, CA: Consulting Psychologists Press

Wonder J. and Donovan (1984) *Whole Brain Thinking*, New York: Ballantine Books

---